Pseud. Devonia

The Honiton lace book

The second and enlarged edition

Pseud. Devonia

The Honiton lace book
The second and enlarged edition

ISBN/EAN: 9783741189326

Manufactured in Europe, USA, Canada, Australia, Japa

Cover: Foto ©Lupo / pixelio.de

Manufactured and distributed by brebook publishing software (www.brebook.com)

Pseud. Devonia

The Honiton lace book

The Honiton Lace Book:

BEING

THE SECOND AND ENLARGED EDITION

OF

HONITON LACE-MAKING;

AND CONTAINING

FULL AND PRACTICAL INSTRUCTIONS FOR ACQUIRING THE ART OF MAKING THIS BEAUTIFUL AND FASHIONABLE LACE.

By "DEVONIA."

WITH ILLUSTRATIONS.

LONDON:
"THE BAZAAR" OFFICE, 170, STRAND, W.C.

LONDON:
PRINTED BY ALFRED BRADLEY, 170, STRAND, W.C.

PREFACE TO THE SECOND EDITION.

THE kind manner in which my little treatise on the art of Lace making has been received, has encouraged me to publish it in a revised and enlarged form. I have made a few verbal alterations in the earlier patterns, as in the course of frequent working, better and quicker modes of doing them presented themselves, still the first part is substantially the same as when originally written. In the second part I have endeavoured to enlarge the area of Honiton lace, and vary the interest, by reviving some of the many different combinations of stitches in which the workers delighted in the old days when Lace-making was at its zenith, before they sunk to the weary round of turkey's tails, spread eagles, conventional roses, vulgar lilies, coarse thread, bad work, and little pay. The concluding instructions are devoted to a form of Lace which is a novelty in England, though it has been long worked in Brussels; I mean the process of doing flowers in relief, by means of which the white threads may be formed into a veritable work of art, and afford scope alike for genius and for high mechanical skill.

I must here add one word of thanks to my kind and talented coadjutor, Olive, without the aid of whose clever drawings it would have been impossible for me to have rendered my descriptions intelligible.

"DEVONIA."

"*The Bazaar*," OFFICE,
   32, WELLINGTON STREET, STRAND.

PREFACE TO THE FIRST EDITION.

In OFFERING to the world this little book upon the art of Lace making, which has hitherto been held a sort of trade mystery into which very few ladies have been initiated, I have been actuated by two motives. The first being the thought that in these high-pressure days, when brains and energies are taxed to the utmost, anyone who contributes to the number of calm and quiet occupations for women is a real benefactor to the sex; and the second being the desire to place within the reach of patience as well as wealth, the loveliest fabric that ever set off female beauty.

I have taken very great pains to make these elementary instructions quite clear. I am aware how difficult the task is to learn a perfectly new process, even with the aid of illustrations, from written words only; but some of my unknown pupils, by sending me specimens of their first efforts, have shown me that it can be achieved, and I therefore greatly hope that I have succeeded in giving a most fascinating employment to many who would not otherwise have been able to attain it.

"Devonia."

"*The Bazaar*" Office,
    32, Wellington Street, Strand.

Honiton Lace-making.

CHAPTER I.

On its Origin and Requisites.

As the taste for lace, the most graceful and beautiful of all feminine adornments, has increased so much lately, so also the pretty art of making it has become widely spread among ladies; but numbers have hitherto been deterred from attempting pillow-lace from the want of instructions, and also from the difficulty (out of the lace districts) of procuring pillows and bobbins. As I have been a lace-worker for many years, I thought it lay within my power to obviate the first difficulty by bringing out a series of instructions for Honiton lace-making; and the second lessens naturally as the ardour for learning increases, since supply will always follow demand.

The Devonshire, or as it is commonly called, the Honiton, lace, is the most beautiful and valuable of the English laces; and it is at the same time the most interesting to make, and the easiest for an amateur to bring to perfection, for whereas the edging laces require a distinct learning for each pattern, and continue in one dull routine, the lace maker, who has once mastered the six stitches of which Honiton is composed, can work out the most abstruse design with perfect ease, and vary it to suit her own fancy.

The old Honiton was copied from the Flemish, and they are so much alike that even an expert finds it now difficult to pronounce decisively which is which; but Honiton has long acquired a distinctive character of its own, and it has the rare merit of not being imitable by machinery, at all events at present; so that even the grosser male intelligence, which is apt to look upon all laces whether hand or machine made "as very much the same," cannot possibly take Honiton for anything but real.

The qualities requisite for learning this lace are delicacy of touch, fairly good eyesight, patience and perseverance, which two last qualities are essential to success in every pursuit whatever.

I have said "fairly good sight," for, although it is not so trying to the eyes as is commonly supposed, still it might prove troublesome to a short-sighted person. The passement patterns and covering cloths should be coloured, the former brown, the latter blue or green; and I would not advise working by candle or lamp-light, as the pins throw a shadow which is apt to be confusing. Beginners are very apt to tire their eyes, because in their eagerness they look too intently, and so strain the sight, as a learner of knitting often strains her thumb, by concentrating her attention upon her work, and in consequence holding her needle too tightly; but practice improves the faculty of touch to so great a degree, that the fingers of an experienced knitter or lace maker will detect a mistake before the eyes do.

I now come to the paraphernalia required before commencing the study of Honiton. The list is as follows: A pillow (which is slightly different in shape from those used for the edging laces), a cover for the same, two cloths to cover the work, a hank of lace thread, and one of the shiny thread called by lace makers "gimp," four dozen bobbins, a paper of lace pins and one of common pins, a small soft pincushion, which had better have a tongue so that it can be pinned to the lace pillow and shifted at pleasure; a needle-pin, a most useful little implement, which is best formed by heading a darning needle either with a bead or sealing-wax, it is used for pricking the patterns, winding up the thread when the bobbins get too long, &c.—the sewings used formerly to be made with the needle-pin, but a very fine crochet hook is now often used for that purpose; a bobbin-bag, which should be not quite so deep as the bobbins, and stitched down in compartments only large enough to take a dozen pair at a time; a pair of scissors which will cut sharply at the points, and finally a passement pattern.

The simplest and, as I think, the best mode of arranging the pillow, is to cover it with soft white linen or calico, and make the cover cloths of blue or green batiste or calico. As Honiton ought to be kept of snowy whiteness, it is desirable to have two sets of pillow covers of a washing material.

Undoubtedly, however, if ornament is looked to, the prettiest material is silk, and it is pleasant to work upon; but satin is bad, and velvet entirely inadmissible, that is, if real work is intended; it is hard to stick the pins into, and the bobbins drag upon it in a most unpleasant manner. The dimensions of the cover cloths should be 18in. or 20in. by 12in. One is used for covering the work already done; the other, the pattern that is to be worked over in order to prevent the threads from catching in the heads of the pins which fasten the pattern on the pillow. When not working, one of the cloths should be turned lightly over the pins, to preserve the lace from dust. Everything is to be pinned on the pillow, and not fastened in any other way, for Honiton does not follow one steady course, like the edging lace, but moves in eccentric orbits, continually requiring the pincushion, covers, &c., to be re-adjusted.

As the work, however, is all done on the top of the pillow, it rather improves its appearance (as an article of furniture) to give it a flounce or valance about 4in. deep.

When all these articles have been procured, and the pillow dressed, the next thing to be done is to wind the bobbins, which operation is to be performed as follows :—Hold the bobbin in the left hand, and wind from you with the right; keep the winding as smooth as possible, but do not over fill the bobbin. When sufficiently full secure the thread thus; holding the bobbin still in the left hand, with the palm upwards, and the thread in the right, place the middle finger of the left hand upon the tightened thread; a turn of your wrist will now bring the thread round your finger; transfer the loop thus formed to the bobbin by gently pulling with the right hand while you put the loop over the head of the bobbin with your finger. This is called a "rolling or half hitch," and keeps the bobbin from running down. The thread can be lengthened by tightening it, at the same time gently turning the bobbin round towards the left; or shortened by lifting the loop with the needle-pin and winding the bobbin up. When wound, the bobbins must be tied in pairs by fastening the ends of the two cottons, the ends of the knot out off as closely as possible, and wound a little way on to one bobbin, the other being unwound proportionately; this is in order to get the knots out of the way for the first start, as they are very troublesome things, and have to be dealt with in divers ways, which will be duly enumerated at the proper time. Winding with a machine, when possible, is to be preferred to hand-winding, as the latter is apt slightly to discolour the thread, even when the greatest care is taken.

CHAPTER II.

On Whole Stitch—Plain Edge.

HAVING prepared the bobbins, you can now commence the first pattern, thus :—Take the pillow on your lap, resting it against a table or chair to steady it; fasten on the *passement* pattern by running two or three common pins straight into the pillow through the edge of the pattern; pin the cover-cloths across, so as just to leave exposed between them the leaf you are about to work. Stick a lace-pin into the pinhole at the top of the leaf as far into the pillow as will steady it, and hang twelve pair of bobbins on to this pin; the length of the thread from the bobbins to the pin should be about four inches. Arrange the bobbins so as to have those which contain the knots in the middle. The bobbins are always treated in pairs; there is but one exception to this—the gimp bobbins, which will be spoken of after-wards. They are divided into two classes, working and passive. The latter should lie straight down the pillow, not in a heap, but slightly spread out in a fan shape; the workers, of which there are always three pair, work across the passive ones from side to side alternately. Do not number or in any way mark the bobbins; they are so continually changing that it will only confuse you to do so, but in your own mind call the pair you are working with 1 and 2, and the others 3 and 4, 5 and 6, 7 and 8, &c., as you come to them. One word as to the management of hands and eyes. As soon as possible get the habit of using both hands simultaneously, to assist in which I will give directions as to which hand is used. Delicacy of touch is, as I have said, an essential, for lace thread is so brittle; at the same time the touch should be firm, and there should be continual tiny pulls, especially at the edge.

For the eyes, accustom yourself to watch the work, and not the bobbins, and then you will be able to detect a mistake at once; otherwise you do not find it out till the end of the row. I will now proceed to give directions for whole or cloth stitch and plain edge.

Fig. 1. Leaf in Progress.

First, run the lace pin down to its head to hold firm the 12 pair of bobbins; twist the outside pair on each side 3 times to the left; put the left hand pair aside, and take the two next pairs, numbering them 1 and 2, 3 and 4. 1 and 2 are the working pair, and will work across, taking the other bobbins as they come.

1st stitch. Put 2 over 3 with the left hand; with both hands put 4 over 2 and 3 over 1; 1 over 4 with the left hand; push away 3 and 4 with the left hand, and bring forward 5 and 6 with the right.—2nd stitch. 2 over 5 (l. h.); 6 over 2 (r. h.); 5 over 1 (l. h.); 1 over 6 (l. h.). Push away 5 and 6 (l. h.); bring forward 7 and 8 (r. h.).—3rd stitch. 2 over 7 (l. h.); 8 over 2 (r. h.); 7 over 1 (l. h.); 1 over 8 (l. h.). Push away 7 and 8 (l. h.); bring forward 9 and 10 (r. h.).—4th stitch. 2 over 9; 10 over 2, 9 over 1; 1 over 10.—5th stitch. 2 over 11; 12 over 2, 11 over 1; 1 over 12.—6th stitch. 2 over 13; 14 over 2, 13 over 1; 1 over 14. 7th stitch.—2 over 15; 16 over 2, 15 over 1; 1 over 16.—8th stitch. 2 over 17; 18 over 2, 17 over 1; 1 over 18.—9th stitch. 2 over 19; 20 over 2, 19 over 1; 1 over 20.

You have now worked across to within one pair. To do plain edge, twist 1 and 2 three times to the left with the left hand, while the right is taking a lace pin from the pincushion; then, holding both bobbins in the left hand, stick the pin in front of the twisted thread into the first pin-hole on the right hand as far into the pillow as will hold the pin steady, give a very small pull to draw the twist up; this had better always be done after a twist. You have now two pair outside the pin. The right hand pair you find twisted, as it was done at the commencement. Make what is called

ON WHOLE STITCH—PLAIN EDGE.

the "stitch about the pin," 2 over 21, 22 over 2, 21 over 1, 1 over 22. Twist both pairs 3 times to the left, using both hands simultaneously; pull the twists gently up. The first pair have now worked across, and are put away, the last pair becoming 1 and 2 in their turn; but before commencing this row I must give a word of caution. In the first row you took the bobbins as they came; in arranging them so as to make the knots belong to the passive bobbins, they were of necessity twisted over one another. At the beginning this does not matter; but now each bobbin has its separate place, and every twist will show a defect in the work. It is here that the quality of patience comes into play. In putting a pillow down the bobbins are very apt to run together and become twisted; but they must be carefully disentangled each time.

Half a beginner's work is to recover the bobbins from a tangle. It is a tiresome process, but not a difficult one; and it has its uses, as it gives facility of handling the bobbins, and accustoms the eye to detect the wrongful twists.

In the 2nd row the bobbins must be numbered from right to left, 4 and 3, 2 and 1; the latter being the working pair. There is an apparent reversal of the stitch, but in reality the theory is the same, *i.e.*, there are two pair of bobbins concerned, a right and a left hand pair; the middle left hand bobbin is always put over the middle right hand one, each of the latter pair is put over the one nearest it, and the middle left hand again over the middle right.

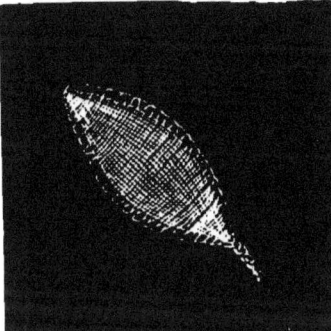

FIG. 2. LEAF FINISHED.

In working from left to right the workers begin and end the stitch; in the return row the passive pair begin and end it. I will now give the second row, the bobbins being numbered thus: 22, 21, 20, 19, 18, 17, 16, 15, 14, 13, 12, 11, 10, 9, 8, 7, 6, 5, 4, 3, 2, 1.—1st stitch. 3 over 2 (l. h.); 2 over 4 (l. h.); 1 over 3 (r. h.); 4 over 1 (l. h.) Put away 3 and 4 with the right hand, bring forward 5 and 6 with the left.—2nd stitch. 5 over 2; 2 over 6, 1 over 5; 6 over 1.—3rd stitch. 7 over 2; 2 over 8, 1 over 7; 8 over 1.—4th stitch. 9 over 2; 2 over 10, 1 over 9; 10 over 1.—5th stitch. 11 over 2; 2 over 12, 1 over 11; 12 over 1.—6th stitch. 13 over 2; 2 over 14, 1 over 13; 14 over 1.—7th stitch. 15 over 2; 2 over 16, 1 over 15; 16 over 1.—8th stitch. 17 over 2; 2 over 18, 1 over 17; 18 over 1.—9th stitch. 19 over 2; 2 over 20, 1 over 19; 20 over 1. You have now returned to the edge, and find the pair of bobbins which were put aside at the commencement of the first row; twist 1 and 2 thrice to the left, stick a pin in the first left hand pinhole (in front of the twist); make the stitch about the pin, 21 over 2; 2 over 22, 1 over 21; 22 over 1, twist both pair thrice, and pull the twist up. Repeat these two rows until you come to within three rows of the end;

then cut off a passive pair in each row, close up to the work, but taking great care not to cut the working thread. When the leaf is quite finished, divide the bobbins into three divisions, and plait them for about a quarter of an inch; this is called "The Beginner's Stem." Take the two outside bobbins, turn their tails to one another, and tie them by passing one over, one under the opposite thread and drawing through, this is done twice, and is called "tying up." Tie two or three more pairs to keep the plait from undoing, and cut close off. Take out the pins; tie the bobbins in pairs again, wind away the knots, and do another leaf.

To recapitulate the instructions. Use both hands. Look at the work, and not the bobbins. Always twist to the left. Stick the pins in only far enough to hold them steady. Keep the bobbins of an even length, and the passive ones spread like a fan. Undo all tangles.

Good lace looks fine and compact, the pin-holes are close together, and the edge firmly twisted. In bad work, on the contrary, the edge looks ragged, and the pin-holes are far apart and straggling, which gives the lace a loose and coarse appearance. It is as easy to do good work as bad, and the result is far more satisfactory.

CHAPTER III.

ON KNOTS AND GIMP.

THE question of knots and broken threads must now come under consideration, as they are sad stumbling-blocks in the learner's path. If a casualty occurs in the passive bobbins, it is easily repaired; a knot must never be worked into lace under any circumstances, but if there is one inconveniently near, all you have to do is to lift the bobbin, draw the thread back over the work, and either twine it in and out among the pins until you have passed away the knot, or stick a pin in the pillow behind the work and carry the thread round that, taking care not to pull it unduly tight, and bringing it down again straight to its proper place; lengthen the thread, which, as I said before, is done by tightening it, and turning the bobbin to the left, and continue the work. In the case of a broken thread it is managed in this way. Cut the end off close to the work, stick a pin behind the leaf in a straight line or nearly so; wind the new thread five or six times round it, make a loop, which pass over the head of the pin, and bring the bobbin down to its proper place. The working bobbins

ON KNOTS AND GIMP.

require a little more particularity in dealing with them; if you find you have a knot in one you must change it away by giving it one twist with either of the bobbins next inside the pins, there it will not show, but in the middle of the leaf it would. By this process the knotted thread becomes passive, and in the course of three or four rows may be dealt with as above directed. If a working thread breaks, you must undo the row until you come to the side where it was lying idle; cut the end off close to the pin, fasten the new thread to a pin straight behind the work, and tie the pair by turning their tails to one another, and drawing them, one under and one over the opposite thread twice, taking great care to draw up the first tie quite close to the pin, and unless you have the securing pin in a straight line, this is rather difficult to do. If both working threads break short

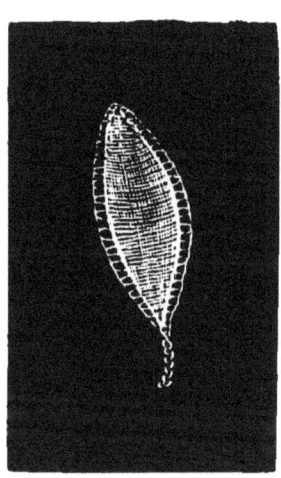

FIG. 3. REMOVAL OF KNOTS.   FIG. 4. LEAF WITH GIMP.

off, a beginner had better consider the leaf spoiled, and take it off at once, but if one thread is long enough to knot up temporarily, it can be "changed away" the first opportunity, and the other one may be tied at the edge. Do not deal with several knots in one place, always manage to have two or three rows between. The extra threads should not be cut off till the leaf is finished. In working tendrils or small circles, they sometimes have to be cut off soon, as the pins are in the way, but that is generally in stem stitch, which holds the thread tighter, and there is not the same danger of their drawing out.

Gimp is the coarse glazed thread which is sometimes seen inside the edge of leaves and flowers. It gives stability to the lace, and is often used as a substitute for the raised work at the side of leaves, being much more quickly done. There are several ways of applying the gimp, but 1 will deal with them separately, as occasion arises, not to load the memory with details which cannot be worked out at once. The simplest mode is as follows.

Fill two bobbins with gimp, and make the half hitch as directed; tie them together, and wind away the knot on one. They are to be used separately, but they are fastened together in order to put them on. Commence a leaf as before, using the same number of bobbins. A gimp bobbin is to lie on each side, immediately inside the pins, and is passed through the working pair each time. Thus, in the first row, from left to right, the gimp is put over No. 2 and under No. 1 to begin, and under No. 2 and over No. 1 to end the row. In returning from right to left, the gimp is passed under No. 2 and over No. 1 at the beginning, and over No. 2 and under No. 1 at the end. When the leaf is finished, cut the gimps off before plaiting the stem.

CHAPTER IV.

On Stems and Sewings.

Stem stitch forms an important part of Honiton lace, for not only are the stems and tendrils made with it, but also the circles inside flowers, and the raised work at the side of leaves, &c.

The little flower in the illustration is formed entirely of stem stitch; and in working it I shall be able also to teach another important process in this lace, that of sewing.

Stick a pin at the end of the stem, and hang on six pair of bobbins. This is the usual number for the stem; in some very fine ones, five and even four pair only are used, but unless directed to the contrary, it must be understood that stem stitch is to be done with six pair. You will observe that the pin holes run on one side of the stem, and it is on the stitch at the inner edge that the variation is made, the rest is done in whole stitch and plain edge. To proceed, give the preliminary three twists to the outside pair, and put them aside; with the next pair work across till you come to the last pair; make a stitch and a half (or turning stitch) as follows: work a whole stitch, give each pair one twist to the left, put the middle left-hand bobbin over the middle right; lift the two pairs with each hand and give them a little pull to make this inner edge firm; put aside the inner pair and work back with the other to the pins, when make the plain edge with the pair which had been first put aside. Stem stitch must always be on more or less of a curve, and the pin-holes must be on the outside, so that it is sometimes necessary to turn the plain edge from the right to the left hand in the course of the work; but the turning stitch is always the same, i.e., one whole stitch, each pair twisted once to the left, middle left-hand bobbin over middle right, pull up. You will find that the innermost bobbin works backwards and forwards, but that the second one of the pair remains stationary.

In working round sharp curves you should slant the pins outwards; and if you run one down to its head every here and there, three or four upright ones will be sufficient to hold it steady, but where the stem is nearly straight more upright pins will be required. You can easily pass away knots in stem stitch, and the extra threads may be safely cut off after five or six rows. When you have worked round the circle inside the flower you will find that you are coming across the stem, when you must make a sewing before doing the plain edge, thus: stick a pin into the pin-hole above the one you wish to sew to, as the work requires to be held down firm for sewings. Insert the crochet hook into the vacant pinhole, and under the twisted strand at the left hand side of it; draw one of the working threads through in a loop, pass the second working bobbin through this loop tail foremost, pull the loop down. Take out the securing pin at the side, put it into the sewing hole; make the plain edge stitch, and continue the work as before round the first petal, here you make another sewing, but with a slight difference. In the first place you make it with the inner pair of bobbins, and on this occasion the turning-stitch is dispensed with; you work straight across, sew to the nearest pin hole, but to the outside edge instead of the strand across, which you will find rather easier; work straight back, and continue stem stitch round the middle petal. The pins rather interfere with one another where the curves are so near, but after the first row you can take them out of the finished work. At the end of the middle petal make a sewing like the last, but at the end of the third, where the work is finished off, two will be required; the first to be made before the plain edge stitch is done, the second after you have worked back to the inner edge, and this last sewing must be made to one of the cross strands, and is a little troublesome to do. Then tie all the threads inside

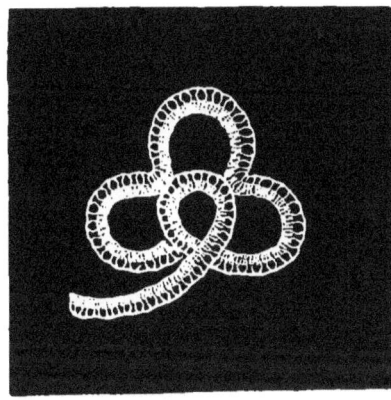

FIG. 5. OPEN TREFOIL.

the last pair, tie up two or three more pairs, and cut off quite close. The sewings and tyings up are the reason of Honiton bobbins being made so plain; for the other laces the bobbins are turned and ornamented with beads, but the Honiton must be perfectly smooth, as they are continually passing through loops. Some old-fashioned lace makers prefer the needle pin to the crochet hook for making sewings, and there are places where it is necessary to use it; when you do, keep the thread tight till the needle pin has hold of it, then slacken it, and give a little flick with the needle pin, which will bring the loop through the pinhole. The little trefoil spray is a pretty one for sprigging nets, but all the examples I am giving are parts of a large spray, and they can either be used separately or put together afterwards.

CHAPTER V.

ON LACE STITCH, HANGING ON BOBBINS, AND FALSE PINHOLES.

THE next stitch to be learnt is a very pretty one, half or lace stitch; and we will return to the original leaf pattern, as that gives space enough to master this stitch thoroughly. Stick a pin at the tip of the leaf, and hang on eleven pairs, run the pin down to its head: it should be understood that this is always to be done when fresh work is commenced, therefore I need not repeat the direction every time. Work the first row in whole stitch; this again is always done at the commencement of lace stitch—it is to bind the threads down in their proper places. Now give each pair one preliminary twist to the left, except the three working pairs (which of course have been already twisted three times) and also the pair immediately inside the pins on each side; these two pairs are never twisted, and a whole stitch is made as the workers pass them at the beginning and end of the rows, which forms the streak you may observe running down each side of the leaf, and therefore I shall call it the streak stitch.

The principle of lace stitch is that only one bobbin works across the leaf each time. You treat the bobbins in pairs, but the working pair is continually changing, therefore one thread runs straight across, and the others slant down the work cross-wise. The stitch itself is as follows : Make the whole or streak stitch, put the pair aside, and give the working bobbins one twist to the left, bring forward the next pair, which are already twisted; put the middle left-hand bobbin over the middle right, twist both pairs once to the left; bring the next pair forward; middle left-hand over middle right, one twist with both pairs, and so on until you come to the streak pair; make a whole stitch without twisting (as at first), twist thrice and make plain edge; then return in the same manner, being careful always to make one twist after the whole stitch has been done, a thing which learners are very apt to forget. When within a few rows of the end, cut off a pair; in this stitch, however, bobbins must not be taken off indiscriminately as in whole stitch, but cut in pairs, being tied up first. Finish off with beginner's stem.

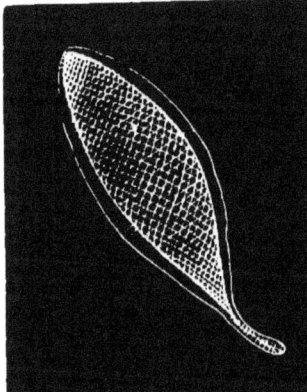

Fig. 6. Leaf in Lace Stitch.

It is a little difficult to deal with knots in lace stitch, therefore they should be wound out of the way; but if an unlucky one should appear it may be treated in this manner: tie it up with its pair, cut the knotted thread off, fasten the new one round a pin, and bring it down to its place; then tie up again. This must be done very neatly, as defects show so much in lace stitch. Never take a knotted thread across if you can help it; it is easy to avoid doing so by giving an extra twist at the edge. The bobbin with the knot should be the foremost one in doing the streak stitch, and then the twist sends it back. Of course a knot can be managed at the edge, as that is in all respects the same as directed for whole stitch; but the fewer threads that are tied at the edge the better, as it is so difficult to cut the ends close off.

Fig. 7. Close Trefoil and Leaf in Lace Stitch, with Gimp.

In Close Trefoil there is no new stitch to learn, but it will give an opportunity of practising all those which have been described, and also two operations which are frequently resorted to in Honiton, viz., hanging on fresh bobbins in the course of the work, and making "false pin-holes."

Commence at the end of the stem. Work straight up it (the leaf will be done afterwards) and round the inner circle of the flower, making a sewing where you cross the circle. We now come to the petals, which are done in whole stitch; but whereas there are more pin-holes round the outside edge than there are on the inside, which constantly happens round a curve, the system of false pin-holes here comes into play; but before describing them I must explain how to increase the number of bobbins, as those you have on will not be enough round the thick part of the flower. You may, however, work the first two rows with the six pair, then just before sticking the second pin on the outside, take another pair (the knot having been wound away from the middle), pass the thread underneath the two workers, run it up close to the passive bobbins, stick a pin, and complete plain edge. You have now a seventh pair, hanging on to the threads which come across, work two more rows, and hang on another pair in the same manner.

By this time it will be necessary to make a false pin-hole, in order to keep the outer and inner edges level with one another. Work across to the inside, twist thrice, and stick a pin; but instead of completing the edge, come back with the same pair; when you again return to the inside, take out the pin, and re-stick it in the same hole, then finish plain edge with the idle pair. By this means you stick two outer pins for one inner, and bring the work smoothly round the curve. Where pins stand very close together, twist only twice instead of three times, or the edge will be puckered.

The false pin-holes must be repeated until you have rounded the petal, and come to the thinner part, when you must cut off a pair, choosing two knotted threads. As you turn the corner to the second petal, sew twice to the circle, hang on two pairs in two following rows, and cut them off when you have rounded the petal. The third will only require one extra pair hung on, so there will be eight pairs for the first and third petals and nine for the middle one, which is rather wider.

When you have finished the third petal, sew at each side, tie all the threads up inside one of the working pairs, then tie them up separately, and cut quite close.

In working this pattern remember to turn your pillow as the work turns, so as to keep the passive bobbins straight in front of you; if you neglect this the threads draw to one side. When you hang on the six pair at the commencement you had better leave three or four knots near the work and change them away as you pass up the stem.

For the leaf you must hang on eight pair and two gimp bobbins. The latter will take the place of the streak stitch, which is now omitted, the gimp being passed through the working pair on each side; in all other respects this leaf is to be worked in the same manner as the large one; as you approach the stem tie up two pairs (in successive rows) and cut them off; sew to the stem on each side; cut the gimp close, tie the remaining bobbins inside the working pair, then tie them separately and cut off.

CHAPTER VI.

On the Difficulties of Beginners, and Finish of Leaf.

I TRUST that those ladies who are doing me the honour to follow my instructions, are becoming more at ease with the bobbins than they were at the commencement of their task. In all instruction it is best to begin by explaining first principles, without distracting the attention with many minute directions as to mere matters of detail: but the time is now come when I can give a few hints which may smooth away the difficulties of beginners, and enable them to work with greater rapidity and precision. I have observed that these difficulties are principally five : making the twist, drawing up the threads, unwinding and winding up the bobbins, and doing the sewings. I will take them in the order in which they come. First the twists : a beginner generally makes them by turning the bobbins over and over one another on the pillow in a careful and laborious manner, whereas the experienced lace maker lifts the pair in her hand, holding them loosely, and twists them with a rapid action of her fore finger and thumb; it will seem awkward at first, especially making both twists at once at the edge, but a little practice will soon give the knack, and it is worth acquiring, as it saves so much time. The second difficulty is in making the tiny pulls of which I have before spoken ; learners are apt to fall into one of two extremes, they either pull up the threads at every stitch, which is not necessary, and sometimes pull so hard as to break them ; or, for fear of the latter, they do not draw them up at all, and then the work looks loose and ragged. In whole-stitch you should pull up in three places ; after the first stitch, when the row is finished (just before the pin is stuck), and after the three twists are made. Stem stitch requires careful drawing up, especially round curves, and not only the workers but the passive bobbins at the inner edge should be pulled and patted to draw them down tight. Lace-stitch, on the contrary, does not want much pulling, except at the edge.

Simple as the operations of unwinding and winding-up the bobbins appear, they give a good deal of trouble to learners, as the threads ought all to be kept the same length, and therefore need continual adjusting. To shorten it, lift the bobbin with the left hand. holding it horizontally, raise the loop or hitch with the needle-pin, and hold it out while you wind up the bobbin. To lengthen the thread, tighten it, and slowly turn the bobbin to the left ; if it refuses to run, there is nothing for it but undoing the half-hitch by lifting it over the head of the bobbin, and making it again when the thread is the proper length. New bobbins are very troublesome in this way, especially when the thread in the course of the winding touches the head of the bobbin; I suppose the wood, being new, is slightly rough, for I find no difficulty with my bobbins, which are polished by the work of many years, but on the new ones, wound for the first time, the thread continually sticks.

All these, however, are but minor troubles which a little practice will soon obviate; but the fifth on the list, the sewing, is the most difficult part of Honiton lace, and you should take great care in doing it at first to prevent getting into a slovenly way about it. It certainly is very provoking to poke and poke in a futile manner for a quarter of an hour, and finally to break the thread, which involves undoing the work for some way; but perhaps the following hints may avert some disasters of this sort. Before doing a sewing you should remove the pincushion, all extra pins, or anything which interferes with the free movement of the hand; hold the hook lying along the pillow until you have hold of the thread, then bring it to an upright position, and draw the loop through with a series of little wriggles. You should always bear in mind that whether you are sewing to a cross strand or outside edge, the hook is to be inserted into the pinhole and not into the vacant space at the side. Do not sew with a knotted thread if you can possibly help it, it does not matter which of the workers you use; if, however, a knot is inevitable, as sometimes happens, do not draw it through into the pinhole, it is so apt to break as it comes down again.

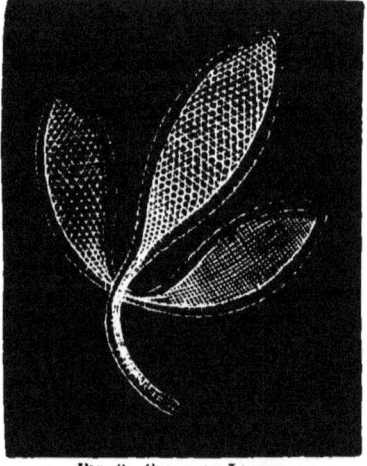

FIG. 8. SPRAY OF LEAVES.

If you have tried at a strand several times and failed, and it is beginning to get frayed, sew to the strand on the other side the pinhole, or even to the outside edge, anything is better than making a hole in the lace; at the same time these expedients, especially the latter one, should only be resorted to in cases of extremity, as they draw the edge in and show a blemish.

For doing the sewings with the needle-pin, I will give more detailed instructions when we come to the raised work.

I will now proceed with the instructions for making the spray of leaves (Fig. 8).

In this first design, which I am giving in fragments, I am only teaching flat work; for you should be thoroughly familiarised with the various stitches, before you attempt the raised; but when the latter is not used, it is sometimes necessary to cut off the bobbins at the end of a leaf. The simple resource of careless and slovenly workers is to tie them all up, and cut them off, leaving the raw ends like a little brush; others plait beginners' stem from one leaf to another, but this also has an awkward appearance. I hope none of my pupils will be content with doing any but the best work, although it may involve a little degree more trouble. The correct way of fastening off at the ends of leaves is shown in this spray. Begin at the end of the stem, and work down to the middle leaf, which is to be done in lace stitch, with the streak down each side; when you commence it, you must hang on two pair on one side, and three on the other, making eleven pair in all. Always be careful when you turn from the stem to either lace or whole stitch, to twist the pair which is at the inner edge three times at the first pin.

Work down the leaf till you have only three pin-holes on each side, then tie up a pair, and cut it neatly off; do this in each row, and in the last row cut two, so as to leave only four pair.

When you have stuck the end pin, make the stitch about it, and twist the outside pair, but not the second; in this pair tie up all the others very close and neatly. Take out all the pins except three on each side (running one down to its head every here and there); turn your pillow round, first altering the two end pins, and slanting them outwards, bring the threads in between these two end pins, and lay them down over the leaf. Lift the pair in which you tied them up, and pass it round the other threads, take out one of the end pins, but not the one which was put in last; make a sewing, re-stick the pin, pass the same pair round, make another sewing in the next pin-hole, tie up and cut off.

By this means the finish comes on the wrong side of the lace, and the leaf looks all right on the other side; but you must be sure to slant the two end pins, or when the bobbins come back, the end pulls in.

For the two other leaves, commence at the tip of the uppermost, which is also to be done in lace stitch. Hang on eight pairs and two gimp bobbins; a gimp is considered equivalent to a pair, and you must therefore allow more bobbins when you do not use it. Work down the leaf, cut off three pairs (in three following rows), at the bottom; change to whole stitch as you work over the stem, and make a sewing on each side. Continue with the number you have for the first three rows, then hang on a pair each row for four rows; and this hanging on must be done at the end of the row, but before the gimp is passed through the working pair, for the gimp must always lie next to the pins. Finish off this leaf in the manner before directed, cutting the gimps off before you bring the bobbins inside. This finish requires care and neatness, but the effect quite repays the additional trouble that is expended on it.

CHAPTER VII.

ON THE DEVONIA SPRAY AND FIBRE LEAF.

HAVING now made all the different parts of the spray, except the main stem and one leaf, it only remains to put them together, which is done by pinning them down in their several places, and sewing each to the main stem as you pass up it, the open trefoil being sewn separately to the leaf spray. You may, however, if you please, treat these leaves and flowers as distinct sprays, and work the one given in this article as a whole, which I would at any rate advise when you rework it, as it is the easiest way of doing it.

I have called it the Devonia spray, because it does not represent any particular flower, for I could not attend to botanical accuracy in the design, as each part had to illustrate a special lesson. In to-day's work there is still something to be learnt, the fibre stitch, and then the Devonia spray will be complete.

In working it as a whole, you must begin with the main stem; hang on nine pair and a gimp, which latter runs up the outside of the curve. Work in whole-stitch, and as the stem narrows, cut off a pair of knotted threads here and there, until, as you near the leaf, you have only four pair and the gimp remaining. A false pin-hole will be required where the stem bends. When you commence the leaf you must hang two pair on the gimp side, and two pair and a gimp on the other side. The leaf is worked in whole-stitch, but a fibre runs down the middle; this is formed by the workers being always twisted before and after doing the centre stitch; for the first four rows twist them once, then twist them twice until you come to the widest part of the leaf, when twist thrice for two rows, then twist twice, and as the leaf narrows to the point only once. In the last three rows, cut off three pair, tie up the gimps, cut close off, and finish at the tip as before directed. Now hang on six pair for close trefoil, sew the outside pairs to two adjoining pin-holes in the main stem before you begin the trefoil stem.

The spray of leaves is next to be worked, joining to the main stem in the same way, by sewing the two outside pairs. When a stem is commenced in this way, there is no necessity to run the first pin down to its head, as the sewings assist in keeping the bobbins firm. In making the third leaf it will be as well to connect it with the close trefoil leaf, and this is effected in the following manner: when you have stuck a pin in the hole nearest to the leaf you wish to connect to, before doing the stitch about the pin lengthen the thread of one of the workers; sew to the leaf with this thread, and pass the bobbin through its own loop; stick a pin in the sewing hole (I trust, by the way, that this is never forgotten in doing sewings, for the work pulls dreadfully when it is), bring the thread back to the leaf in progress, make the stitch about the pin, wind up the bobbin, and proceed. Now work open trefoil, joining it to the leaf spray ; and last of all come the large leaves which formed the primary lessons. In making these, I would recommend an extra pair being hung on to each. I purposely allowed rather too few at first, as, though it makes the work coarser, it shows the effect more clearly ; but the greater the number of bobbins, in reason, the finer and better the lace looks. Work the lace-stitch leaf first, hanging on twelve pair; connect it with the fibre leaf at the nearest place, take off three pair of bobbins at the bottom of the leaf ; sew twice to the main stem ; plait across it, and sew again to the other side. Continue with the same bobbins for the whole stitch leaf, but add two pair on each side ; connect this leaf with close trefoil, and finish off at the tip. Lastly, work the gimp leaf, which you will commence at the tip ; cut off the bobbins as the leaf narrows ; to finish off, sew twice to the main stem, tie up all the bobbins in the last pair you sewed with, then tie separately in pairs, and cut off.

This last leaf may be omitted if you like, and when again working the spray, you can alter the disposition of the

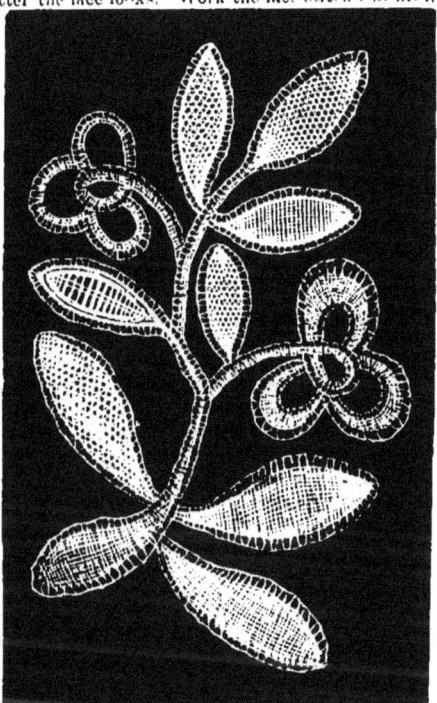

Fig. 9. Devonia Spray.

stitches in the various leaves at pleasure. It is, I think, one of the great charms of Honiton lace, that you can vary according to fancy. Of course, the edgings, like other edging laces, must be worked in regular routine ; but for the sprays, you may work in whole or lace stitch ; make the leaves with or without a fibre; use gimp or not ; do flat or raised work at your will; and what you do once you need not do again. You must bear in mind a few facts, namely, that whole stitch requires one or two more pairs than lace stitch does ; that for the fibre you must have an uneven number of passive pairs; and that each gimp, as I before remarked, stands in place of a pair; but your eye will soon become accustomed to judge how many bobbins are wanted. It is astonishing in looking over old lace, to observe how the makers revelled in variety of detail, thereby obtaining a richness of effect, which we, with our modern notions of uniformity, rarely attain.

CHAPTER VIII.

ON PEARL EDGE.

THE subject of the present lesson will be the pearl edge, of which there are two sorts, the right and the left hand pearl. Those ladies who already know any of the edging laces are probably acquainted with the left hand one, therefore in this pattern I will teach the right hand, giving the other at some future opportunity.

Hang on ten pair at the end of the leaf; work it in whole stitch: cut off four pair, and go round the inner circle in stem stitch; sew as you cross the circle, and commence the first petal of the flower. Work it in whole stitch, hanging on two pair in successive rows, and making false pin holes where required. The edge will be plain as usual until you have passed the point of contact with the next flower; then commence the pearls, turning your pillow so that the edge which has hitherto appeared to be on your left hand will now be on your right. The working pair (being at the inner edge) must come straight across, and be twisted once before doing the last stitch; then without sticking a pin, make a whole stitch with the pair that are lying outside the pins, pull up; twist the workers seven times, to the left of course; lift one of them in the left hand, taking a pin in the right, place the pin under the thread, give a twist with your wrist to bring the thread round the pin, run the pin up to the hole, stick it, lay down the bobbin, and pass the other one round the pin from the lower side, *i.e.*, the side nearest to you, twist once; make a whole stitch, again twist once, and work back. You will now find that you have only two working pairs instead of three; continue in this manner, making pearl edge on one side, and plain on the other to the end of the first petal, when sew twice to the inner circle. The lowest hole at the bottom of each petal just where the work turns, should be made in plain edge and not pearl. Work round the middle petal, sew twice; then for the third, make seven pearls, and then

ON PEARL EDGE TREFOIL.

turn to plain edge, and in doing this, do not omit twisting the outside pair three times at the first stitch. As you narrow down, cut off a pair; connect to the leaf at the nearest place, and when you reach the inner circle sew to it; then make what is called a rope-sewing down it to the next leaf, and that is done as follows: lift all the bobbins but the pair you sewed with, pass this pair round the others, sew to the next hole, pass the pair round again, and so on until you reach the leaf, when disentangle the bobbins, and hang on two pair if you work in lace stitch, three if in whole stitch. Work down the leaf, connecting to the first petal at the nearest point of contact: at the bottom of the leaf cut off two or three pair according as you have knotted threads. Make stem-stitch for two pinholes; and repeat from the beginning, the only difference being that in all

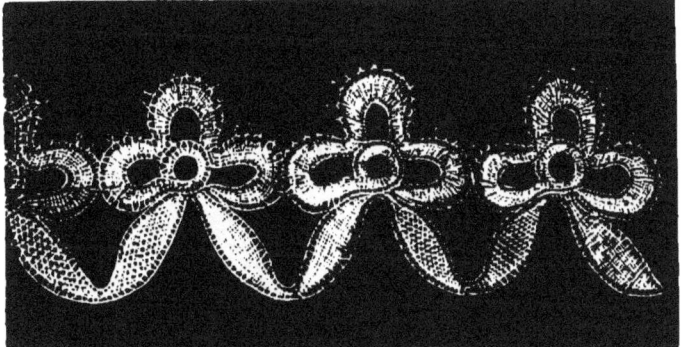

FIG. 10. PEARL EDGE TREFOIL.

the following flowers, when you come round the third petal, you sew twice to the preceding flower where it touches. If you wish to continue this edge, you must move the bobbins in the following manner: turn the flap of the cover cloth over them, and pin the doubled cloth tightly on each side, also pinning it to the cushion so that the threads shall be a little slack while you take out all the pins from the finished portion.

Now detach the cloth containing the bobbins from the lower end of the pattern, and fasten it down again at the upper end; pin the last made trefoil and leaf down on the first, putting pins half-way up the leaf; undo the bobbins and continue working. The illustration shows the stitches to use. A footing braid (see Chap. xiii.) should be added, unless this pattern be used for edging net.

The special things to be remembered in doing right hand pearl edge are: to put the pin under the thread; to pass the second thread round the pin from the lower side; and to twist once before the last stitch and after the first in the return row, which makes a line of demarcation between the pearls and the body of the work, and greatly improves the effect.

CHAPTER IX.

Raised Work—Needle-pin Sewings.

We have now arrived at the most difficult parts of Honiton lace, and those which require very careful work. I give only a portion of a design in this lesson—a spray of leaves, to teach raised work; the flower which accompanies it, and which will be engraved in the next chapter, will contain the last of the Honiton stitches proper—the plaitings; all others are modifications of the stitches already described, or belong to different laces. The raised work is the distinguishing mark of Honiton, and its crowning glory. In no other of the English laces is it introduced, and the value of a piece is estimated according to the amount of raised work in it.

It is the part which most tries alike the eyes and the patience; but by the process I have given of ending off at the tips of leaves, it can always be dispensed with by those who find they cannot master it satisfactorily.

Commence at the end of the stem, leaving several knots near the work, to change away as you pass up it, and winding the others well out of the way. When you reach the middle leaf, change the side for the pins, and continue the stem up the lower side of the leaf till you have stuck the last pin but one. Take the passive pair which lies next the pins; lay it straight back over the work, and do one row of stem without it. At the last pin hang on four pairs, letting them lie down by the side of the pair you have put away; make the stitch about the pin, and do one other row of stem stitch with the bobbins you have been working with; come back to the edge; then turn your pillow quite round, so that the bobbins lie down the leaf facing you. Take out all the pins but the last three, and work straight across in whole stitch. The last stitch will be done with the pair you put away; tie this pair once, and work back with it. You will now continue working in whole stitch, making plain edge at one side of the leaf, and doing sewings to the cross strands of the stem at the other. My own experience

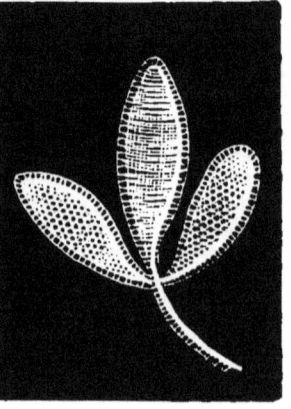

Fig. 11. Spray for Raised Work

is, that whereas it is infinitely easier to do all connecting sewings with the hook, still, in a long series like this the needle pin is preferable. One must keep all the pins in down the leaf, which hamper the hook, and cause it to get entangled in the strands. I will therefore give directions for doing the sewings with the needle pin; but for those who find the hook easier the only difference will be that the lower securing pin must be omitted. To proceed, having worked back to the stem side, make a sewing thus: stick a securing pin in the hole below the one you are going to sew to, so that there will be a hole vacant between two pins; lay one of the working threads across this vacant space, holding the bobbin in your left hand. Insert the needle pin under the lowest strand, and insinuate the thread underneath it, which is easily done if you hold the thread tightly down with your fore finger. Directly you have hold of it slacken the thread, bring the needle pin over, keeping the thread under the point; then give a little sharp flick, and the thread will come through in a loop; draw this loop farther through, and hold it with the needle pin while you put the other bobbin through it. Take out the securing pin, stick it in the sewing hole, and work back with the pair which made the sewing. This process is repeated every row, but when you get near the bottom of the leaf, where there is generally a little turn, the hook may be used again. As the leaf narrows, cut off four pairs, choosing of course the knotted threads.

You may, if you please, tie up all the bobbins in one pair after doing the last sewing, and cut them off, recommencing at the next leaf; or you may make a rope-sewing down the stem, which saves both time and thread to those who do not find the sewings too difficult. When you reach the next leaf (the uppermost one) disentangle the bobbins, and work the stem up the upper side. This leaf is made in lace stitch, and will therefore only require three pairs hung on at the top; in all other respects the directions are the same as for the first leaf. Cut off the three pairs at the bottom of the leaf, cross the stem, but you need not make a sewing in doing so; carry the stem up the lower side of this leaf, hang on three pairs (or four, if you prefer working in whole stitch), work down it as before, and at the end tie the bobbins up in the last sewed pair, and cut off.

CHAPTER X.

Long Plaitings.

Now we come to the plaitings, which are, as I have before mentioned, the last of the Honiton stitches. I do not mean to say that they are confined exclusively to Honiton, for they are used largely in Maltese and other laces, and the little dots in Valenciennes grounding are made in this stitch; still they are Honiton stitches, *par excellence*, and my instructions would not be complete without them. There are three sorts; the long (sometimes called diamond when they cross one another) the square, and the broad, which latter are commonly called cucumber plaitings, from a supposed resemblance to cucumber seeds. Plaitings are principally used for filling the interiors of flowers, and are generally the last part of the spray to be done. It is so in this instance. The flower must be made first, and the directions are as follows: Work a stem with five pair only round the outside edge of the circle, keeping the pins on the right-hand side; when you have come round, hang on two pair, join the ends; work across in whole stitch, hang on another pair. Work round the circle again in whole stitch, sewing each row at the stem side as directed in the last chapter. These sewings can be done with the hook, as there is no long straight row of pins to interfere with it. When

FIG. 12. LARGE DAISY.

you have again completed the circle, join the inner edges; work across, cut off two pair, and with the remaining six commence the petals, which are done in stem stitch. Here, again, is a slightly different process to learn. You will observe that the last two holes belong equally to the petal on each side; work round the first petal until you come to these holes, stick a pin in the first, complete the edge stitch, then lay back by the pins the outside pair. Work across, and, as you come back to the pins, twist thrice

LONG PLAITINGS.

the passive pair lying next them, and make the edge stitch with these, but do not twist the active pair which you leave lying at the pins; work across, sew at the inner edge to the circle, turn your pillow, work back to the pins where the untwisted pair is lying; do not touch the pins, but work across and back with this pair, and when you return to the pins, take out the second one, sew to the hole, restick the pin, and do another row of stem. All this is done without twisting, and you have now arrived at the commencement of the next petal; twist the outside pair thrice, stick a pin, and finish the edge stitch with the pair which had been put away, thus returning to the original six pair.

Every petal is the same, and when you have finished them sew to the first, tie up the bobbins, and cut off. Now, for the plaitings to fill up the centre of the flower, you will notice that there are four detached holes, and four in a group in the middle. Stick a pin in one of the detached holes, and hang on two pair; wind the knots thoroughly out of the way, for nothing can be done with knots in plaiting, and the bobbins therefore require careful handling to avoid breaking the threads. Connect to the flower by drawing a thread through the nearest hole, and passing one of the other pair through it; take out the pin, and stick it in the sewed hole, make a whole stitch, twist each pair twice, and stick a pin in the hole between them. I must now ask you once more to number the bobbins in your mind, 1, 2, 3, 4; 1 and 4 lie down the outsides, some distance apart, 3 down the middle, and 2 passes backwards and forwards under and over them, changing from one hand to another. The theory of the stitch is this:—

1st row—2 over 3, and under 4.
2nd row—2 over 4, under 3, and over 1.
3rd row—2 under 1, over 3, and under 4.

The two last rows are repeated until the plait is long enough. The hands are managed thus;—You lift 2 with the left hand, and 4 with the right; put 2 over 3 and under 4, passing it into the fingers of the right hand; drop 4, and bring 2 back over it; now lift 3 with the left hand, pass 2 under 3, and into the fingers of the left hand in the same manner; drop 3, take 2 over 1, lay it down on the pillow, and turn 1 over it with the left hand; once more bring it over 3 and under 4. Every three or four turns pull 2 gently up to make the plait tight; if in doing so you draw it in, pull 1 and 4 simultaneously, which will bring it out again to its proper size; it is also as well to give a little pat to No. 3 occasionally. The beauty of a plaiting consists of its being the same width all the way down and very smooth. When you have reached the cluster of holes in the middle, twist both pairs twice, still handling No. 2 very gently; stick a pin between, and leave them. Hang on two more pair at the detached hole opposite the first, and bring another plaiting down to the centre, sticking a pin between the pairs. Make a stitch with the two pairs that lie next one another between the pins; twist each thrice, and carrying the respective twists in front of the pins, make a stitch with each outside pair; twist thrice, make a stitch with the two inner pairs, thus completing the square, twist, stick two pins, and continue the plaitings. Bring the left hand one down to the detached hole opposite it, and after sticking the pin and making the stitch sew to the flower, tie up, and cut off; finish the other plaiting in the same manner, and the flower will be complete. The leaves may either be made before or after, and will be connected with the flower by the little bit of stem. Plaiting is a rather difficult process to master. You must not try to work too quickly at first until you have got the knack; hold No. 2 with the thread slack, and be careful when you draw it up, and do not change it for any other of the bobbins. Beginners sometimes get confused by the twist under 1, and bring back 1 instead of 2, which is fatal. Unpick ruthlessly if your plaiting looks rough at the edges, for nothing spoils the effect of a spray more than bad plaitings.

CHAPTER XI.

RIGHT AND LEFT PEARLS—CUCUMBER PLAITINGS.

THIS design is intended as a study of plaitings. I have put a pearl edge to it for the purpose of teaching the left pearl, but I would recommend those who find a difficulty in the plaitings to work the butterfly with a plain edge the first time, as the sewings are rather easier.

The body and head must be made first; commence at the tail, hang on seven pair and two gimps; work in whole-stitch to the place where the pattern narrows, when cross the gimps underneath the bobbins, and continue the upper part of the body; when you come to the head, cut off two pair of bobbins, and tie up and cut off the gimps; work stem round the head, and sew and tie up to finish. Make a rope-sewing to where the right hand wing begins, and hang on another pair. Work stem along the upper part of the wing; if you make a pearl edge, twist twice before the last stitch, and after the first in the return row; this is to make a more decided line of demarcation, and is necessary when a pearl edge is put to a stem, as the stem draws up so much closer than the other stitches.

Continue the stem round the circle at the end of the wing, changing to plain edge where it turns inside; make a sewing where it joins, and tie and cut off all but two pair; make a stitch with these, twist twice and stick a pin between them in the nearest single hole. Fill the circle with plaitings according to the directions given in the last chapter. Now return to the body of the butterfly to do the close part of the wing: hang on five pair and two gimps, sew each outside pair to the body; work in lace stitch, hanging on a pair at the slanting side for six rows. When you have passed the point of junction with the lower wing, commence the pearl edge, which will now be a left pearl ; the difference between the two is simply this ; in the right pearl you form the loop by placing the pin under the thread, and you carry the other thread round the pin after it is stuck from the lower side, moving the thread to the right first. In the left pearl you place the pin upon the thread, and bring the bobbin over it with the left hand, then you run this loop up to the hole, stick the pin, and bring the other bobbin round the pin from the lower side, moving first to the left. The difference seems slight, but it is necessary to remember it, for if the pin is put the wrong side of the thread, or the second thread passed round the reverse way, the edge untwists, and looks ragged. At the end of the lace stitch part a pair should be cut off in each of the two rows before the end one, and three pair in the end row ; the one side is, of course, to be joined to the circle by sewings where they touch, a final sewing made at the end, the

FIG. 13. PEACOCK BUTTERFLY.

bobbins tied and cut off. For the lower wing, again commence at the body, hang on six pair, and work the band of whole stitch round the wing, beginning with plain edge, and turning to pearl just below the tail. From the place where the wings join, sew each row to the upper wing, dispensing with the edge stitch on that side.

The left wing is to be done in precisely the same manner; and then fill in the plaitings. The diamond ones, which fill the lower wings, are done in the manner already described at length. There are, of course, more of them ; but, as the illustration will explain this, and they are all done on exactly the same system, I will not take up your time with a repetition of instructions, but will merely mention that you commence at the upper part of the wing, and that you will require six pair of bobbins in all.

The cucumber plaitings must now be learnt, and it is these sewings which will be made more easily to the plain edge the first time. With either edge they must be made to the cross strands, and if you have not been very careful with the twist to make the line of demarcation, it is a little difficult to find the cross strands in the stem, especially the first one or two sewings. Have ready nine pair with the knots wound well away; stick a pin into each pearl as far as the sewings extend, as the loops may otherwise draw in. Hang on one pair at the second pearl, twist it four times, and two pair at the fifth (which will be opposite a hole), make a stitch with these last, twist twice, stick a pin, make a stitch about the pin, twist four times; then make a plaiting with the first pair and the one nearest to it, leaving the third pair idle for the present. Keep No. 1 and 4 very wide apart, so as to make the plaiting a broad one, and hold No. 2 very slack. After the first two rows, draw 2 quite up, and then pull out again with 1 and 4, this will tighten the original twist, but you must never pull 2 again; when it has passed backwards and forwards about six times, twist it with No. 1 four times (which will make 1 the outside bobbin). Sew 1 to the lace stitch, and pass 2 through it, but be very careful in handling 2; an unwary pull to that bobbin will spoil the plaiting. Now hang on two pair more opposite the next hole, make a stitch, twist twice, stick a pin, make a stitch about it and twist four times; then make another plaiting with the pair which was originally left idle, and the one nearest it : you can still call the bobbins 1, 2, 3, and 4. For this and the succeeding plaitings, 2 must be passed to and fro eight times; then twist four times, and very cautiously make a stitch with 1 and 2 and the 3 and 4 of the last plaiting, which by-the-bye should also be twisted four times. You may give 3 and 4 a gentle pull, which will bring the other plaiting into place, and pull 1, but not 2. Stick a pin, twist twice, make a stitch, twist four times. Again, one pair may be sewn to the lace stitch, and left. Hang on another couple of pairs at the next hole, and make a plaiting in the same manner, securing the worker and its pair with a stitch as before.

Hang on the two remaining pair, make a plaiting with one, twist the other four times, sew it to the circle, twist four times again, which will bring that pair down in readiness to make the securing stitch of the fourth plaiting. There will be two more plaitings required below to fill up the space, and when all the threads are sewn to the lace stitch, tie them up and cut off. Commence at the farthest end of the other wing, for in these plaitings one pair always has to be idle until the next plaiting is finished, and brings a pair to meet it and make the securing stitch; and that pair had better not be 1 and 2.

Great gentleness and care are required in doing the cucumber plaitings, especially in handling No. 2, but you may keep a firm hand on 1,.3, and 4; the bobbins must be handled very gingerly while the securing stitch is being made, but after the pin is stuck, and the stitch made about it, all is safe. To finish off, make the antennæ with five pair, commencing at the head.

CHAPTER XII.

Raised Half-leaves—Strand Ground—Cutting Bobbins in Pairs.

This pattern is intended to be worked with a plain edge, but a pearl can be put to the stem side if desired.

Commence at the little knob of the stem, work with six pair round the circle then to the flower. Work round the inner circle with five pair, then do the petals in whole-stitch, carrying a gimp round the outside; hang on three pairs in three successive rows, and cut these off as the petal narrows on the other side. At the bottom of each petal lay back a pair one hole before the end, as directed for the daisy, and take it up again when you have turned the corner. When the first flower is finished, cut off the

Fig. 14. Wood Sorrel Pattern.

bobbins and hang six pair on again at the knob of the stem. For the leaves, work round the inner circle, carry the stem down the middle of the first leaf, and come back with whole stitch and raised work, hanging on four pair at the top of the leaf, and cutting them off as it narrows; make a rope sewing down the leaf at the back of the stem; where the leaf parts work stem, hang on four pair, and finish the leaf in lace stitch. Work the two other double leaves in the same way, making a rope-sewing on the circle to the place each starts from; finally cut off the bobbins. It will improve the centre of the flower and the circle to have a cucumber plaiting in them to form a spot, this is not given in the design, as it can very well be omitted. If you put it in, you must do it thus: take two pair, sew them at opposite sides of the top of the circle, twist each four times; make a plaiting, keeping it broad, and well in the middle, twist four times again, and sew the strands to corresponding opposite places at the bottom of the circle; sew No. 1 first, and put 2 very gently through it, then sew 3 and 4, tie both pairs, and cut off. If you cannot manage this sort of plaiting satisfactorily, it will easily cut out again.

Four of these lengths would make either a head-dress, or the end of a neck-tie; with the Devonia Spray in the centre. In the first case, they should be arranged in an oval shape; in the second, as a square; work single flowers for the corners, or for the turn of the oval. Tack the sprays firmly on blue paper, the right side downwards, and do the grounding. There are various ways of grounding Honiton, both on the pillow, and with the needle. I will give the pillow groundings first, and the easiest is what is called "strand ground." It is done with one pair of bobbins, which are sewn to one edge, twisted as much as necessary, and sewn to the opposite side. The strands had better be arranged quite irregularly, and it will be as well to draw on the paper first where they are to come. When you cross another strand sew as you pass, and when you do not wish to start from the place you have last sewn to, twist the threads, and carry them over the lace to the next point of departure; being at the back of the lace this will not show on the other side, but be careful not to pull the strands so as to pucker the sprays.

As this pattern involves a great deal of cutting off bobbins, I will here teach a mode of doing it which will tie them in pairs, ready for hanging on again, and will save time and trouble in consequence. Lift the pair to be tied in the left hand, and place the scissors, closed, under the threads, which bring round over them: then turn the scissor points facing the pillow, open them as wide as you can, and draw the upper threads in between them; if you get them in as high up as the hinge, and then close the scissors gently, the threads will not be cut. Now draw the scissors down out of the encircling threads, and you will find a loop come through on one point of the scissors; snip this, and the bobbins will be tied together.

CHAPTER XIII.

HEADINGS AND FOOTINGS.

IN order to keep the instructions on a level, I must give very simple ones in this chapter. When elaborate sprays and edgings have been made, they need the assistance of braids, otherwise called footings, and small edgings (or headings), in putting them together to make collarettes, ties, &c. These braids and edgings are very cheap, and can easily be bought by those who do not like the drudgery of making them; but some ladies prefer doing the whole of their work themselves, and I will therefore explain a few of the simplest forms of headings and footings. There are larger and more elaborate sorts, which will be described, with the special designs to which they belong:

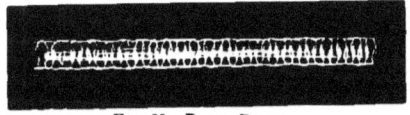

FIG. 15. PLAIN BRAID.

No. 1. Plain braid needs no further description than that it is made with eight pair of bobbins in whole stitch and plain edge.

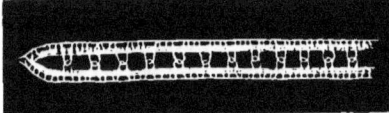

FIG. 16. OPEN BRAID.

No. 2.—Open braid requires twelve pair; one row of stem is made on each side, then (the working bobbins being at the inner edge) twist each pair twice, make a stitch, stick a pin in the centre hole, twist twice, and make the stitch about the pin, then twist twice again, and once more work stem on each side for the space of two holes, when repeat the centre stitch.

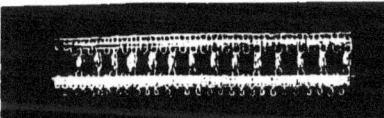

FIG. 17. CUCUMBER BRAID.

No. 3.—Cucumber braid is wider, but does not need more bobbins, five pair and a gimp being sufficient on each side, if a plain edge is made; and if one edge is pearled, only four pair and a gimp on that side. This braid requires more detailed description than the others, as it contains what is called the inner pearl stitch. Hang on the two sets of bobbins, the gimps being on the inside. Begin at the plain edge first, work into the middle, pass the gimp and make the inside pearl by twisting the working pair six times, sticking a pin into the inside hole, and working back with the same pair. Return to the middle, twist the working pair twice, then work the other side in the same manner, only making a pearl edge. Fill the centre with a cucumber plaiting, and when you have finished it, twist 1 and 2 twice, stick a pin in

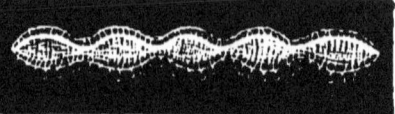

FIG. 18. BEAD EDGE.

the pillow to hold those threads steady, while you twist 3 and 4, and work back to the edge with them; then carry 1 and 2 to the other edge. Make the inside pearls as before, and continue until a sufficient length is made.

For the headings the simplest one is what is called the bead edge; it is made with seven pair and a gimp which runs along the plain edge side; at the end of each bead head twist the gimp twice round all the bobbins but the two pair lying at the plain edge.

The shamrock edge is made with six pair: work down the upper part of the left hand lower leaf in lace stitch, making a pearl edge to the point of contact with the next pattern, turn the pillow, and do the other half of the leaf in whole stitch, sewing every row in the middle,

FIG. 19. SHAMROCK PATTERN.

except the first, which will be secured by taking up the idle working pair lying at the pins. Work the middle leaf in the same way, doing the whole stitch part first, and putting a pearl to both sides; then work the third leaf, doing the lower side first, and pearling the upper part of the leaf. As there are not quite so many holes down the middle as on each side, a false pin hole will be required at the top, and that will bring the bobbins round neatly.

Work stem to the next pattern, and repeat. It will improve this pattern to make a small inner circle.

CHAPTER XIV.

Wild Rose Pattern—Inner Pearl—Raised Fibres.

This pattern, which forms a very pretty edge to a tucker, or border for a handkerchief, affords a good opportunity of practising raised work, and also teaches another method of doing leaves in halves.

Commence at the flower, work the inner circle with five pair, then do the petals, either open as in the design, or close, sewing each row to the edge of the circle, and making the petals alternately in whole and lace stitch, this latter work has the best effect; eight pair and a gimp will be required, lastly fill in the plaitings. There is an error in the engraving as to the pearls, they are better put at the flower side of the pattern, and the straight edge can be sewn to a braid or footing net. Work down the stem with six pair and round the knob. This is for the first pattern; the succeeding ones will commence at the knob. After passing it work stem

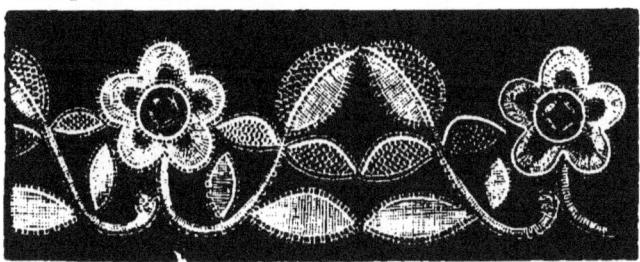

Fig. 20. Wild Rose Edging.

till you reach the leaves. The small leaf touching the flower must be made first; carry stem up the side, and come back in whole stitch with eight pair, connecting to the flower at the point of contact. Next work the large leaf in the same way with ten pair. Cut off four pair at the end, and work the stem to the end leaf; cut off a pair, and continue the stem down the middle of the leaf; hang on two pair, turn the pillow, and work the half-leaf in whole stitch and raised work. At the bottom of the leaf cross the stem, cut off a pair, turn the pillow again, and do the other half in lace stitch. Cut off another pair at the tip, and work the fibre stem down the other leaf, turn at the bottom, and work it in the same manner, and with the same number of bobbins. When you have finished it continue the stem with six pair to the next flower, which work in the same manner as the first, cutting off the bobbins at the end. Then fasten on six pair at the stem and do the two lower leaves, the largest first, joining it at the tip to the other, tie up and cut off at the end of the little leaf. Lastly, work the four middle leaves. If you do them in raised work you must fasten on at the main stem, and make each couple separately, joining their tips with a sewing; but you may, if you please, work them with a gimp, in which case you will hang on seven pair, and a gimp at the tip of the end leaf, join it to the flower, and work in lace stitch; hang on two more pair for the centre leaves, work straight across, cut off two pair for the last leaf, join it to the flower with two sewings, and cut off.

I will now give some small sprays, which will be found useful for filling up vacant places, and each shall convey a lesson to be applied afterwards in large flowers. First in this lime blossom I will teach the continuous inner pearl. Hang on ten pair and two gimps at the tip of the hollow leaf, and do whole stitch to the place where the opening begins; work to the centre, stick a pin in the top hole, hang a pair of gimps round it, twist the two pair of working bobbins twice, make a stitch about the pin, and work first down one side of the opening and then down the other. The stitch at the inside edge is the inner pearl, for which I gave directions in the cucumber braid, but to save the trouble of referring back, I will recapitulate. You work to the inner gimp, pass it through the pair, twist the workers six times, stick a pin, pass the gimp through again, and work back. When both sides are finished all but the lowest hole, the two working pairs will meet in the middle; make a stitch, stick a pin, tie the gimps and cut them off, and let one of the working pairs merge into the passive bobbins. Finish the leaf, cut off all but six pair, work round the circle, and do the second leaf in raised work and lace stitch.

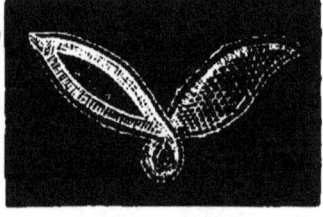

FIG. 21. LIME BLOSSOM.

The next pattern, the half butterfly, gives the inner pearl without a gimp. Do the body first, beginning at the tail; five pair and two gimps will be required. Cut off the gimps at the head, hang on three more pair, and work the antennæ with four pair each. Now hang on six pair at the body, work up the upper wing, hang on four pair, and come back with whole stitch, working the inner pearl as in the foregoing pattern. At the bottom cut off all but six pair; work stem from the lowest part of the other wing for seven holes, then hang on a pair at each hole for four holes, which new pairs are not to be worked in, but to lie back by the pins. When you reach the point of junction with the other wing, sew to it, then work straight across in whole stitch, bringing in the added pairs,

FIG. 22. HALF BUTTERFLY.

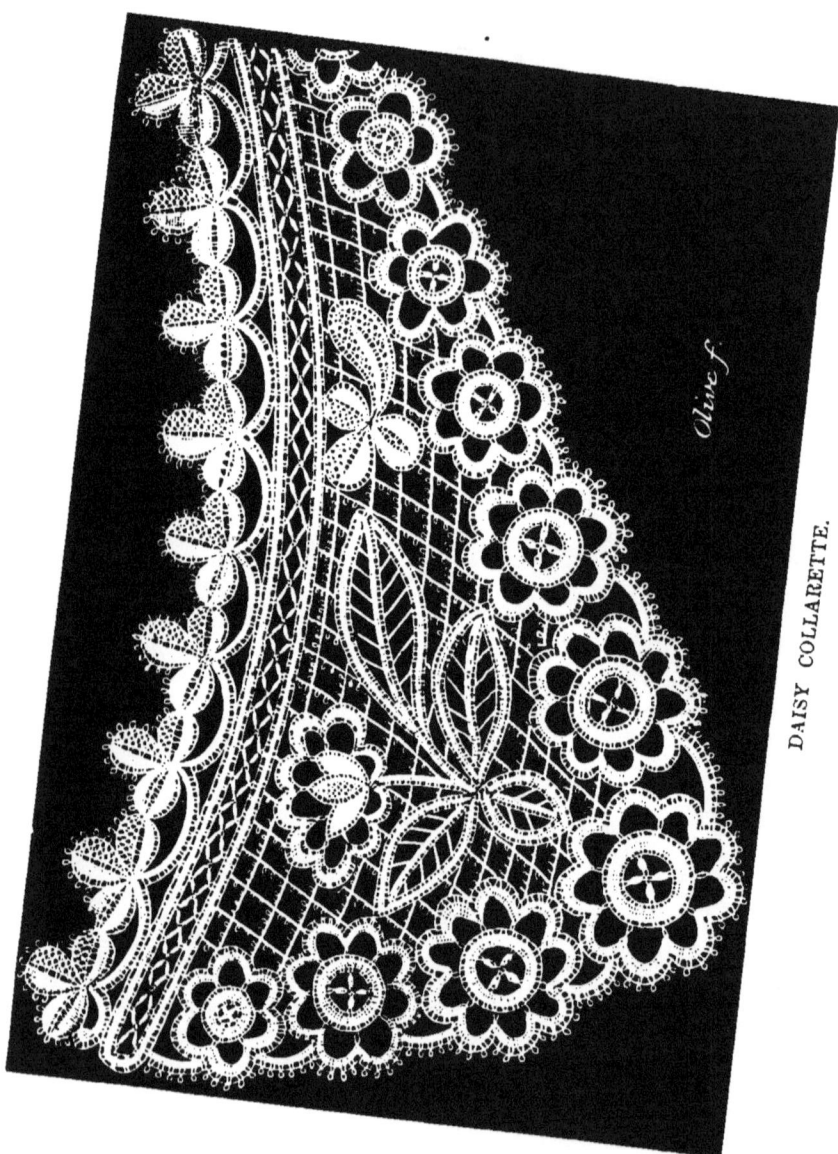

DAISY COLLARETTE.

which must each be twisted twelve or fourteen times. The work will look coarse at first, but will draw into place as the wing narrows.

This next lesson will show the first and easiest method of putting raised centres to leaves, which is called the "centre fibre." Hang on five pair at the stem, work up the middle of the first leaf; when you have stuck the last pin, work to the turning stitch and back, then with the pair lying at the pins, make a rope sewing, and this which is termed a "return rope" is made, not upon the stem, as in former instances, but at the back of it.

Fig. 23. Fibre Leaf.

Work the two next fibres in the same manner, the middle one last, and when you have finished each, run a pin to its head in the end hole and take out the rest. Now carry raised work to the tip of the middle leaf, hang on two pair, work back in whole stitch, and when you come across the fibre, take out the pin, stick it three or four holes lower down, insert the hook into the top hole, and make a sewing with the centre stitch of your work to the cross strand, this will secure the fibre, and you can now work over it. The other leaves may be done in the same manner; or you may omit the raised work, and hang on nine pair at the tip of each, working either whole or lace stitch, and cutting off neatly where they join the stem.

CHAPTER XV.

Daisy Collarette—Branching Fibres—Honiton Ground.

The flowers for the edge of this collarette are made according to the daisy pattern in chapter 10; but they can be worked more quickly if a gimp is substituted for the raised work round the inner circle. In that case stick two pins at the starting point, one at each edge, hang four pair on to the inside pin, and four pair and a gimp on the outside one; work round, connect to each of these places, and then continue as before directed, pearling the edges where it is indicated on the pattern. The little connecting stems are worked afterwards; but a variety may be made, and a deeper scallop given to the edge, by leaving out these stems, and pearling each daisy to the point where it joins the next.

The centre spray shows a different mode of doing the leaves, with open work and branching fibres, which have an elegant effect, and are easily done. Commence at the lowest leaf, hang on five pair at the top of the main fibre, and work stem down it; at the bottom of the leaf hang on another pair, and work the band all round it in whole stitch, joining the middle fibre as you pass it at the top. Now carry the band round one of the adjoining leaves, cutting off a pair when you return to the bottom of the leaf; work the fibre stem up it, join to the band, and cut off. The branching fibres are done in this manner: Sew a pair to the band, near the top of the leaf, twist the threads slanting downwards, and sew to the middle; slant upwards again with a twisted strand, and sew to the opposite band; keep twisting the threads, bring them down over the work, sew to the edge, then slant to the centre again, and so on. The two other leaves are worked in the same manner, but the large one will require seven pair round the band. The flower is so plainly shown in the illustration, that I need not waste many words in describing it: the calyx is done with raised work; the outside petals in stem stitch, and the inside ones edged both sides. Round the neck the collarette is edged with the shamrock and the plaiting braid; the little band on each side of this braid is done with five pair, and the centre filled in with cross plaitings.

The grounding for this collarette is the one that is most commonly used for the best Honiton lace, and is called the Honiton ground. The stitch is merely stem done with four pair and with a pearl edge, worked in squares. Do all the lines one way first, and then the cross bars, making a sewing as you cross each line; these sewings are very easy, you merely draw the loop underneath the line to be sewn to, and pass the other through it. When you reach the lace, make a rope sewing, or plait beginner's stem to the next line, where practicable; but if you must cut off the bobbins fasten with two sewings, and tie up.

If you are arranging a piece of lace to be grounded in this stitch, you should rule blue paper in squares first. Tack your sprays on face downwards, pin the paper on the pillow, and work along the lines.

CHAPTER XVI.

Ivy Leaf Pattern—Open Bead Braid—Net Ground.

THE particular points to be noticed in this pattern are the braid and grounding, the leaves and flowers being very easily described. The middle spray, the heart's-ease, is to be made first, and you begin with the flower. Work the inside circle, then the lowest petal, the inner edge of which will

IVY LEAF PATTERN.

require a false pin-hole at every stitch; this petal will require ten pair and a gimp. The two upper petals are done in raised work; ten pair in the whole stitch one, and nine pair in the lace stitch. Then do the stems with their leaves and buds, which need not be particularised, and lastly the side petals of the flower. Hang on eight pair and a gimp at the point where the lowest petal joins it, and work in lace stitch, finishing at the corner of the upper petal; then work the little bit of stem to the main stalk. The ivy leaves are made with a fibre-stem, a band round in whole stitch, and fibres in Devonia stitch. The footing braid which is called open bead, is done with twelve pair; stem is worked on each side to the place where they join, when the outside pair works straight across and back again, after which the sides diverge once more. I have grounded this pattern in the net ground in order to teach both the pillow and the needle net, though the latter is more used for grounding Honiton lace than the former; I will give the pillow-made net first. It is worked diagonally; and if possible you should begin at a corner, hanging on a pair at each place where a line touches the pattern; and as you hang on your bobbins twist them three times. The stitch itself is extremely simple: put the middle left-hand bobbin over the middle right, thus changing the pairs; stick a pin where the threads cross, twist each pair three times; work thus to the end, then back again. It is very difficult to keep this ground quite as even as machine made net, therefore it is advisable not to have a large unbroken stretch of it; and it is here that the smaller sprays come in so usefully, to spot about and fill up large vacant spaces. If you are arranging lace to be net grounded, I would advise its being done upon tinted paper, but not blue, as the small lines hardly show distinctly enough upon that colour. The lines must be drawn diagonally very evenly, and about the 16th of an inch apart; if they are wider more twists will be required.

For the needle grounding you had better tack the sprays on blue or green paper; it saves the eyes to work over colour, and no lines need be drawn; tack them face upwards and then back the paper with toile cirée or stout brown holland. It is quite necessary to begin this ground in a corner, as the holes do not otherwise pull into proper sexagon shape. Fasten your thread to the lace, insert the needle at about the distance of 1-16th of an inch; bring it out as for Brussels stitch, but twist the thread once round it, so as to make a twisted strand; at the end of each row fasten to the lace with a tight stitch, and sew over and over back again, putting two twists into each loop; sew down the edge the proper distance and repeat.

If you wish a lighter effect, you may make the stitches wider apart and twist the thread twice round the needle.

CHAPTER XVII.

Lily Lappet—Pistils—Strands—Centres—Leaves with Reverse Folds.

To work this lappet, you must commence at the lowest group of leaves, the first being the one showing the reverse side of the leaf. Begin at the root with six pair and two gimps, hang on a pair at alternate sides for four rows; add two inside gimps at the commencement of the open centre, or hollow, and work down each side, the inside edge being plain or inner pearl, according to fancy. As you near the turn, cut off to six pair, work stem down the reverse fold, add one pair and return with lace stitch; when this is finished, cut off all but two pair and fill in the plaitings. Now begin the middle leaf at the tip with six pair and two gimps, hang on a pair each row, so as to have twelve pair in all at the broadest part of the leaf; add the inside gimps at the hollow, and work down each side; at the bottom tie up and cut off the inside gimps, and five pair of the bobbins, thus leaving seven pair and two gimps.

Fasten down five pair and the gimps by running a couple of pins by the threads, slanting crosswise, then turn the pillow, and with the remaining two pair fill in the centre plaitings. Then return again to the bobbins which are left at the bottom, and work up one side of the third leaf and down the other, join to the middle leaf, and cut off all the bobbins. Hang on two pair at the bottom, and do the plaitings. For the back leaves hang on six pair at the tip, and increase each row up to ten pair; the open centre is done by twisting the workers as you pass to and fro, giving an extra twist each time.

The lowest bud is next in order; and, as the two other large buds are done in precisely the same manner, one description will suffice for all. Commence at the tip of the centre fibre, and work to the leaf; come back to the bud with a rope sewing, and work the middle petal in halves. Ten pair will be required at the broadest part of the whole stitch side, and eight pair the lace-stitch; then work the lowest side-petal, beginning with six pair and hanging on two pair in successive rows where it turns down; work the half leaf to the tip, cut off three pair, and do the little reverse half in lace stitch, cutting off all the bobbins at the finish. Hang on five pair for the other side petal, and work it in the same way.

The lily is commenced at the oval of one pistil with five pair, work round it, join the edges, continue down the stem, round the inner circle, up the other pistil, and finish off at the oval. Now begin at a side leaf, hang on six pair, and work to the reverse fold, turn and come back with lace stitch, adding three pair; the upper half of the leaf is done with raised work and whole stitch, and ten pair will be required. Cut off four pair as you near the bottom, sew to the circle for a couple of holes, then begin the middle petal. Work it in halves, with inner pearl down the centre; hang on a pair each time you return to the slanting edge until you have twelve pair if you are working the whole stitch side, or ten pair the lace stitch, then cut off as gradually down to six pair, and as you turn at the point you must put a pin twice into the same hole as in false pin-holes; this may have to be repeated twice or three times, according to the closeness of the holes; increase and decrease in the same manner on the other side. When you hang fresh bobbins on in lacestitch it is not done immediately before sticking the pin, as in whole stitch, but before doing the streak-stitch, or passing the gimp, as one continuous line should run down by the pins. Work the other side petal like the first, and then the first back one in raised work and whole stitch; this will require fourteen pair at its utmost width, and as you pass over the pistil connect to each side of the oval. Cut off all at the bottom, hang on six pair where the leaves part, and in other respects work the leaf as the last. Then do the reverse folds in lace-stitch, hanging on seven pair at the tip, and when you reach the body of the petal, sew two pair to each hole, tie up, and cut off.

Next do the piece of stalk which runs from the leaves to the flower. with five pair and two gimps. For the bud opposite the lily, hang on nine pair and two gimps at the centre tip, work the petal in lace stitch, and the side ones as directed for the large buds. Now carry the main stalk up to the drooping unopened bud, which is worked in halves, as shown in the engraving.

There now remains a half-blown bud and a closed one; for the former hang on bobbins at all the tips, seven pair and two gimps at the centre, and six pair at each of the side ones; bring them down to the point of junction, then work straight across with lace-stitch inside the gimps and whole-stitch outside; at the bottom bring the stalk down to the main one and then do the little end bud.

There are certain rudimentary instructions which I no longer think it necessary to give, as, if my pupils have penetrated thus far into the mysteries they do not require continual recapitulations of the A B C of the art; such as turning the pillow with the work, sewing to the cross strands in raised work, and to the outer ones where lines touch; ending (as a general rule) with two sewings, one on each side, and always tying up at the finish; doing rope upon the stem, except where return rope is mentioned, when it is brought at the back of it.

Also, I need not mention for the future, that where edges slant bobbins should be added or decreased gradually, or that inner gimps should be tied up when they are cut off. The next chapter will describe the border and ground of this lappet.

CHAPTER XVIII.

SCALLOP BORDER—DEVONIA GROUND—BRANCHING
FIBRE LEAVES.

THE border to the lily lappet, of which the illustration is given in the frontispiece, is very easily and quickly worked. It contains no point of any special interest, and a very few words will suffice for its description. Five pair and two gimps are all the bobbins necessary. Begin with the stem of the oval, then add the gimps and work the lace stitch; cut off the gimps, and do the pearled scallops, which will bring you to the commencement of the next pattern. They are all done alike, and the plaitings are put in afterwards. The flower which finishes off the bottom of the lappet need not be described. The lappet end only is here illustrated, but of course the scallop borders can be prolonged to any length required.

We now come to the description of the Devonia ground, so called because it is a variation of the Honiton ground of my own devising, and which, with, perhaps, the blind partiality of a parent, I venture to think very pretty. It is worked thus: fasten four pair to the lace at the commencement of a line. First row: work stem, the turning stitch being on the left side. Second row: work back and make a pearl on the right side. Third row: work to the turning stitch, left side. Fourth row: make a turning stitch to the right. Fifth row: make a pearl to the left. Sixth row: turning stitch to the right. Seventh row: turning stitch to the left;

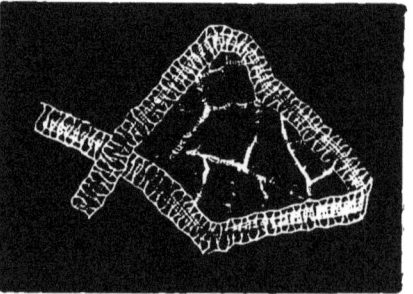

DEVONIA GROUND.

and, eighth row, a pearl to the right again. Thus a pearl is made every third row, on alternate sides, which is capital practice for the right and left pearls. The more irregularly the lines are arranged the better, and when a fresh one starts from that you are working, hang on four more pair before doing a pearl stitch, and leave them behind while you continue the original line: sometimes three or four sets of bobbins are left behind in this manner, and carried on afterwards in different direc-

SCALLOP BORDER—DEVONIA GROUND—BRANCHING FIBRE LEAVES. 49

tions; when you cross a line, sew to it as you do in the Honiton ground. Fasten off very carefully, and, wherever you can, make a rope-sewing to the commencement of the next line. In hanging on the bobbins carefully avoid pulling the lace, and in order not to do so, you should not only stick a securing pin on each side the hole to be sewn to, but also one or two on the opposite side of the lace; then make two sewings into one hole, hanging on two pair at each.

Having finished the lily lappet, the next subject which must engage our attention is the close leaf, with branching fibres.

The leaf shown here is part of a large spray, which will be described in the next chapter; and I would recommend those who are not yet expert at sewings to work this leaf by itself, both in whole and lace stitch,

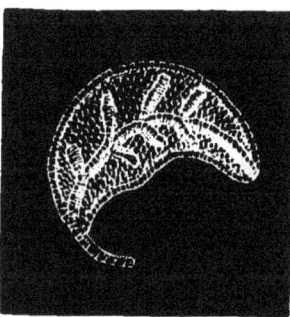

LEAF WITH BRANCHING FIBRES IN CLOSE WORK.

by way of practice. You will commence with the stem, and work to the first fibre; then leave two pair, and work the fibre with four pair, coming back with return rope; do the opposite fibre in the same manner, then continue the main stem, taking up the bobbins that are left. When you have reached the top of the leaf, hang on a pair, turn and work down over the fibres, connecting to the tip of each as you pass it, and twice or thrice to the main stem. If you do the leaf in whole stitch, hang on a pair every other row, till you have sixteen pair; but for lace stitch, add the extra bobbins more slowly up to fourteen pair. Several false pinholes will be required on the lower side of the leaf. You may, if you please, vary this style, and work the leaf in halves, by the following method: Carry the main stem straight up the leaf, stopping just short of the tip; cut off two pair, and come back either with return rope or return stem, which is stem sewn to the back of the first one; the branching fibres are worked on this stem. At the bottom turn and work the upper half of the leaf, sewing to the cross strands of the middle stem and to the tips of the fibres, of course; and then down the lower half, sewing to the same strands. The upper half will require nine pair in whole, or eight in lace stitch; th lower half seven pair in whole, and six in lace stitch.

All my directions have been given for No. 9 thread. If finer thread is used, an extra pair of bobbins should be added for each degree of fineness. No. 12, for instance, would require three more pairs than No. 9.

D

CHAPTER XIX.

CAMELLIA SPRAYS—SQUARE PLAITINGS.

THE directions for making the lower leaves of this spray were given in the last chapter, but in working it as a whole the flower is the first part to be done. It is commenced in the middle with six pair and a gimp, work round the inside petals, then add a pair, and work round again, sewing to one edge, then round again, changing the stitch as shown in the design, add another pair for the outside petals.

When you have finished the last, cut off the gimp and two pair, and work the fibre stem down the front leaf; at the tip hang on four pair, which fasten down on the pillow, and leave. Turn and come back the whole stitch side with the six pair you have been working with, increasing gradually to eight; when you reach the flower sew two pair to each pinhole, tie up and cut off. Return to the tip, work in lace stitch, increasing gradually to six pair; then make a rope sewing to the next leaf, work the half as far as the reverse fold, when turn and come back, finishing at the flower as before; hang on seven pair at the tip and do the reverse fold. The third leaf you commence at the flower, sewing two pair to each pinhole for four holes, work the leaf in halves, finishing at the flower. Lastly, fill in the centre with square plaitings, they require great care in the working as there is no securing stitch between them; the threads are to be twisted twice, instead of four times, and to keep No. 2 from pulling, lay that bobbin with its fellow back on the pillow, resting them against a couple of pins, so that the threads are slack, while you make the next square with 3 and 4 and the pair nearest to them. These plaitings are always worked in slanting lines.

Now begin at the stalk, hanging on eight pair at the tip of the tiny leaf, and cut off a pair as you turn the corner; work up as far as the reversed leaf, hang on five pair, and, leaving six behind to carry on the stalk with afterwards, work stem along the upper part of the right side of the leaf, and the lower of the reverse fold; come back with eight pair, first in lace, and then in whole stitch, cut off. Continue the stalk to the top bud; carry the stem round one side, and across the top of the calyx; add a pair, and work the bud in halves, connecting the first row to the middle hole of the stem. Cut off when you have finished the calyx, and hang on again at the main stalk for the other bud. This is done as delineated, but at the turn of the stem, where the bud springs from the calyx, there should be a pin-hole at the inside edge instead of the turning stitch, which will bring the inner edge into a peak. The three small leaves need no description.

Next comes the largest half opened flower; begin at the bottom of the lowest petal, and work the three middle ones in raised work and lace stitch;

they will require eight pair each; then do the whole stitch back petals, hanging on eight pair at the tip of each.

Now begin at the tip of the lowest calyx leaf with six pair, work that and the middle one, then up the outside petal in whole stitch, and do the open back petals, passing the threads across the one closed petal in a plait. Finally do the third calyx leaf, then the calyx, for which you will require nine pair, as you must work over the middle leaf, and sew to the raised work strands. Cut off three pair and work stem to the main stalk, cross it, and do the hollow leaf, which fill in with plaitings. The other half-opened

CAMELLIA SPRAY.

flower you commence at the tip of the middle calyx leaf, then do the two middle petals, working one over the calyx leaf, which connect at the tip as you cross, then the calyx and the stem to the main stalk. Return to the flower, work the upper calyx leaf, and up the side petal, then the open back petals, down the lower side of the flower, and finish with the third calyx leaf.

The stalk of the flower is then added, and finally the branching fibre leaves, which have been already described, are worked, which finishes the spray.

CHAPTER XX.

NEEDLE GROUNDS—STAR AND DAME JOAN STITCHES.

IN this chapter I shall give two examples of needle grounds; for ladies who cannot make the lace itself will nevertheless find it very interesting to arrange sprays according to their fancy, and ground them by hand. To the minds of those who are used to work point lace a number of stitches will doubtless present themselves, which may be used for this purpose; but I shall content myself with describing the Star and Dame Joan grounds, both of which being as yet unpublished stitches, I cannot be accused of plagiarism. The Star ground has, it is true, very much the effect of one of the Medici stitches in Mrs. Mee's "Point Lace Sampler," but it is worked in a different manner, and is, I think, a little easier to do.

The best thread for grounding is No. 9; any fine needles may be used, but the pleasantest to work with are the long pointless ones. Tack the sprays, as directed for needle-net, on coloured paper or calico, stoutly backed. It is preferable to work these stitches on the right side, as is usually done in point lace; but they can with equal ease be worked on the wrong side, the only difference being that the order of the double Brussels stitch must be reversed.

For the Star Ground commence on the left hand, at the space of one pinhole down the side of the work. Make a buttonhole stitch at the distance of one-eighth of an inch, then a second close to it, thus: Put the needle up through the lace from behind, and bring it down under the thread. This is called double Brussels, and has much the effect of a tatting stitch. Make another double stitch one-eighth of an inch off, and so on to the end of the row. Work down the side to the next pinhole, carry the thread across and fasten it, work down the side again; and then repeat the first row, making double Brussels stitches into each loop, working over the stretched thread so as to fasten it in. The Star Ground is best used for grounding skeleton leaves or very open sprays.

The Dame Joan Ground is an old stitch, which was formerly used a good deal for grounding open laces. It is rather troublesome to work, and also, I fear, to describe intelligibly; but I will do my best as to the latter. It is of a sexagon shape, with a double thread everywhere; like the net, it is essential to begin it in a corner, otherwise it works in straight lines, and will not pull down to the sexagon. Fasten your thread to the side, and make a loose stitch nearly a quarter of an inch off. If you now analyse this stitch, you will perceive that there are two threads, one running up to the lace, the other coming down from it, the needle being on the latter; insert the needle between these threads, and make a tight stitch on the first, that is, on the thread belonging to the loop just made. This makes the double thread on one side of the stitch; continue to the end (if you have more stitches than one), fasten the thread firmly, and work back.

For the return row, make a double Brussels stitch into the centre of each loop, and also over the tight stitch between the two threads, and you will

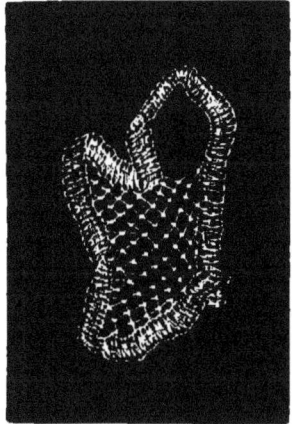
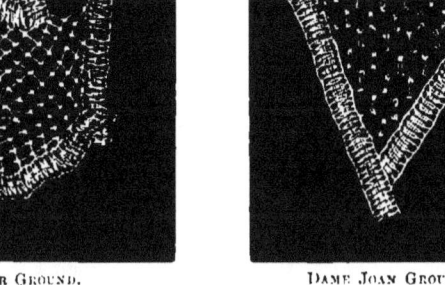

STAR GROUND.   DAME JOAN GROUND.

then find that you have doubled the threads on all sides. In each succeeding row you must work into the double Brussels stitch in the centre of each loop, which pulls it down to the required shape. Dame Joan stitch must be worked firmly, and with a steady hand, it looks untidy if the thread is too loose, and an unwary jerk puts it out of place; when well done, it has an extremely elegant effect.

CHAPTER XXI.

SPRAY OF FERN.

HAVING exhausted the ordinary stock of Honiton stitches, I will now commence to describe the mode of doing several which were formerly introduced into the old Devonshire and Flemish laces, but have for the most part fallen out of use in England; the reason being, as I believe, that in olden days people bestowed more time and thought than they do now. Whether one looks at old carving, embroidery, lace, or any other kind of ornamental handiwork, dating from before the middle of the last century, the same reflection arises that it was more individualised, and that the maker got more pleasure out of his or her work, and took more pains to follow out special fancies than is done nowadays, when everything is made in the fever of competition, and quickness of result is the grand desideratum. Naturally, by the doctrine of selection, the more delicate and difficult descriptions of work disappear, and those only survive which can be done quickly, and have a fair general effect.

In puzzling out these old stitches with lace-makers, I have been more than once met with the remark, " This would never pay to work ;" as, however, my instructions are principally for the benefit of those who make lace for their own pleasure, and do not so much care about its " paying," I propose to revive some of the old modes of working, and infuse more variety into Honiton lace than it at present possesses.

In the following lesson—the fern spray—no new stitch is taught, but it affords good practice for the centre fibre, a process which it will be best to master thoroughly before commencing " tracery," which will form one of the succeeding lessons. Commence at the small curled frond, hanging on eight pair at the centre tip; work round, sewing to one edge as long as the curl lasts; hang on another pair where the spray turns at the bottom; pearl one edge to the place where the small leaves begin to unfold; then make both edges plain and work round to the centre of the frond, cutting three pair off by degrees; when you reach the middle, return with the small opening leaves, making the first one plain, and doing the others with raised work. Make a very neat beginner's plait between each of the tiny leaves, and be careful to sew to the edge at the beginning and end of each; you must also fasten the tip of the leaves to the opposite edge. When you have finished the leaves, tie up and cut off. Now hang on six pair at the place where the narrow stem of the smaller leaf commences, work to the

SPRAY OF FERN.

tip; as you approach the end of the leaf, hang on another pair, and in order to work it in without increasing the width of the stem, pass the extra threads between the pair you are working with, without making a stitch. At the end, turn the pillow, sew a pair to the last hole in order to make the third working pair, and come back in whole stitch, sewing to the centre fibre as you work across one way, but not to the return row. The six small leaves at the end are done in halves, the remainder of the leaves with the fibre. As they grow larger and require more pairs, cast on two or three in the process of working the stem, passing the threads through as before directed; any other pairs that may be required must be hung on at the edge in the usual way. The largest leaves will require about thirteen pairs, as the beauty of the spray depends on the closeness of the work. Plait the threads very neatly between each leaf, cutting off to six pair, of course. Pearl one edge of the wide stalk at the bottom of the leaf; sew each row to the other frond where they touch, work up the stem of the large leaf, and proceed in the same manner as the smaller one.

CHAPTER XXII.

Lessons on Tracery—Emperor Butterfly.

This little butterfly will illustrate the process of "tracery," or a pattern worked over a background of whole or lace-stitch. It was extensively used in the old Honiton lace, and gives a very rich effect; it is not difficult, but is a little troublesome to do, and of course takes longer time. Begin at the tail, hang on eight pair and two gimps; work in whole stitch, crossing the gimp at the narrow part, tie them and cut off at the finish of the head. Add two more pairs so as to have five pair for each of the antennæ; finish them at the tips with two sewings, cut off. Now hang on five pair at the small ring in the lower wing; work round it, joining where it touches, then down to the body; add another pair, and work stem round the inside edge of the lower wing, sewing to the body for the first three or four rows. When you have come round the wing to the body again, sew once, carry the "trace," as it is called, round the oval in the upper wing, then round the inner edge of the wing to the place where it joins the lower one; sew as you cross the trace, and hang on four more pairs, so as to have five on each side for the cucumber plaitings, which are done in this way. Do a row of stem on each side, and when the working pairs come into the middle again, make a cucumber plait; when finished, turn No. 2 bobbin back over the pillow, supporting it with a pin to keep it from slipping; work the stem rows with 3 and 4, and then the plait will not pull up when you work with 1 and 2. Make four of these plaitings, joining the little ring to the edge as you pass it. It is a general rule that all edges must be connected where they touch, so I need not repeat the direction each time. When you have finished the plaiting cut off five pair, and bring the remaining ones back in a zig-zag trace; cut off. Fasten on ten pairs to do the cucumber plaitings in the upper wing, and when completed you may fill up the vacant space, either as in the illustration, with two zig-zag

EMPEROR BUTTERFLY.

traces that cross each other, or with long plaitings, which will be easier. Having done both wings in this manner, you now fill up the back ground. Hang on eight pair to the upper end of the large wing, and work in lace stitch, sewing to each side; add a pair at each sewing, for six turns. As there will be the most holes on the lower side of the wing, you must occasionally sew twice into the same hole the upper side; you will find the needle pin better for these sewings than the hook. Cut off three or four pair as you narrow down to the body; then turn and fill in the lower wing, adding the pairs again; sew securely at the finish. Now cast on five pair at the head, and work the outer edge, pearling all round.

CONVOLVULUS SPRAY.

CHAPTER XXIII.

Convolvulus Spray.—Buckle Stitch.

HAVING described the butterfly, I will now proceed to the leaves and flower, commencing with the spray containing the latter. I shall teach a new stitch in this pattern called buckle stitch, it makes a very good variation for stems.

Commence at the base of the upper leaf with five pair, carry stem down the leaf, making branching fibres on each side, turn and work half the leaf in whole stitch, making the two little holes with inner pearl—ten pair will be required. Cut off to five, take them down to the tip again, with return rope, turn and work the other half leaf. Cut off to six pair, work the ordinary stem to the butterfly, then add two pair, and work the main stem in buckle stitch.

As a rule, this is usually done with eight pairs, four working, four passive pairs; but the number of the latter may be increased if a greater width is required. The stitch itself is simple: for the first row work from left to right into the middle, that is, across two passive pairs; twist the workers once, and also the next pair (which will now become the fourth working pair); make one stitch, twist both pairs again once, continue across to the other side with the first workers, make the edge stitch, and bring them back into the middle, twist once and leave them. Now take up the fourth working pair, work to the left edge, back into the middle, twist once. You now find that there are two pair of workers, meeting in the middle, both twisted; make a stitch with these pairs, twist once, then again work with each to the edges, and back into the middle.

Buckle stitch makes a very pretty braid, and is easier to do than either the cucumber or open braid; leaves may also be worked with it, having the effect of an open fibre down the middle. Continue the buckle stem to the calyx of the flower, cut off two pair, and do the calyx with raised work, cutting off all bobbins when you return to the stem. Now commence at the tip of the first tendril, and, when you reach the stem, cross it, and work the second leaf, cutting off at the end. Hang on again in the middle of the flowers, six pair as usual, work round ; then make little centres to the petals, carrying rope from one to the other. The petals themselves are done in the following manner: work stem up one side to the point of divergence ; continue the stem to the middle of the petal, but hang a fresh pair on every row before completing the edge stitch; put these pairs aside, only working with the original bobbins.

By the time you have added five pair in this manner, you will have reached the centre, turn your pillow, work in whole stitch across the stem, and the last added pair; tie this pair and work back with it in lace stitch, with which stitch you will now continue. Return to the stem side, take in an extra pair, making a whole stitch in doing so, tie and work back.

Thus you will increase a pair each return row, until all are added, and the tyings take the place of sewings; but you must be careful to make the tie stitch a whole one. Continue the petal in the ordinary manner, sewing to the raised side; there may be fewer holes on that side than the other, and it will be, therefore, occasionally necessary to sew twice to the same strand. Fasten the tip of the fibre as you pass it, and also the tip of the tendril when you work the petal which it crosses.

As the petal narrows gradually, cut off to six pair; turn and carry rope to the point where it diverges, then commence again, hanging on the extra pairs, and continue the process I have described till the flower is completed. Now work the leaf and tendril which come from behind the flower, beginning at the tip of the tendril; when you have followed its windings till it reaches the flower, fasten the threads along one side of the edge of the petal, hang five pairs on along the other side; turn, and work the leaf in whole stitch (catching the tendril here and there), and finishing at the tip. The remaining leaves and tendrils are done in the same manner as those first described, and when completed it forms an extremely elegant ornament for the hair, made up with a bow of ribbon.

CHAPTER XXIV.

Convolvulus Spray.—Flemish Stitch.

In this chapter I give the continuation of the spray for the hair, the upper part of which was described above. As the large flowers and some of the leaves are done in the same manner as there described, I will confine myself now to teaching the process of doing the half-opened flowers, and also a new stitch—or rather an old one revived from Flemish lace—which I will call Flemish stitch. After working the first fibre-leaf and its stem to the main stem, bring this latter in buckle-stitch down to the leaf dotted with little holes; this is Flemish stitch. Work

CONVOLVULUS SPRAY.

the fibre stem to the tip with six pair, hang on four more pairs, and add two extra pairs afterwards; work the leaf in halves as before directed; the holes are done in this way; when you come to one, twist the workers twice, stick a pin below them, work to the end; when you again return to the hole, twist the passive pairs on each side of it once, and twist the workers twice as you pass below the pin; this is the whole of the stitch. You can put the holes near or far, according to fancy, and it makes a very pretty variety for leaves.

After doing this leaf, work the two upper flowers; in the flower covered with tendrils, you will do first that which touches the leaf, and then the one running up to the stem; the flowers themselves need no description.

When you come to the first half-opened flower, you will work down to the stem, round the circle, then do rope sewing to the flowers, carry them down one side, every now and then making a double turn-stitch, as the pin holes are on the inner curve. At the end of the stem cast on four more pairs, and work the whole stitch across the flower; turn and work a few rows of lace stitch, sewing one side to the whole stitch; then, with five pair, work stem round the triangle, then once_more commence the lace stitch, and finish the flower with it.

The other small flower is done in a different manner. Work the raised stem as before, hang on three pairs, do about four rows in lace stitch, leave those bobbins; hang on five pair at the further end of the triangle, work round it, then continue in lace stitch, taking up all the bobbins, and finish the flower.

CHAPTER XXV.

Poppy and Briony Designs—Devonia Lace— Serrated Leaves.

WE have now arrived at the final series of instructions, which will teach a development of lace unknown in England until the year 1874, although it has for some time been made in Belgium.

The speciality is that the inner petals of the flowers, the butterflies' wings, &c., are made to stand out in bold relief, so as to imitate the natural forms. As this is not Honiton, pure and simple, and must therefore have a distinctive name I will venture, though with some hesitation,

E

to call it Devonia lace, as I am the first to describe it, although not the only one to have it made in England.*

Beautiful as this lace is in its effect it is by no means easy to do, and I would warn beginners from attempting it; perfect mastery over the bobbins, and ease and facility in drawing the sewings must be attained before entering upon the intricacies of lace in relief. As I am, therefore, writing for those who have made themselves mistresses of their art so far, I need not explain at length each leaf and tendril, the exact number of bobbins, or the precise way in which the parts follow, as a glance at the illustration ought to be sufficient to show these matters.

I will merely give a general view of the pattern, and then proceed to particularise the novelties; for, besides the different ways of working in relief, all of which are here exemplified, several new stitches are introduced, in order to make these, the concluding illustrations of the work, as comprehensive as possible.

The design is a mixture of poppies and briony, with butterflies; the long eaves, which form, as it were, the framework of the pattern, are to be done first; then the inner flowers, leaves, &c. The border is next worked, and the ground filled in; then the lace is shifted on the pillow, to allow of the succeeding scallops to be worked over the same pricking. When the whole is completed it is taken off the pillow, and the parts to stand out in relief finally arranged with a needle.

Having now given a general summary of the pattern, and the order in which the various portions are worked, I will proceed to the details, and the instructions will commence with the long leaves which have jagged or serrated edges. This is a species of leaf which, under different forms, is very popular among lace makers. It looks difficult, but in reality is not so. The first leaf to be worked is the one at the edge with vandyke plaitings in the centre; commence at the base, carry the stem along the inner side to the tip; turn and come back. The first two or three jags are simply made by spreading the bobbins, adding more if necessary, and following the course of the pin holes; but as the indentations become deeper, the following method is resorted to: If you have on, say, eight pair of bobbins, leave the three inside pair, and carry the stem with the others to the tip, hanging on a fresh pair at each pinhole, but leaving it behind; when you reach the tip, turn and work straight back across these new pairs, all of which will be wanted.

This system must be pursued whenever the indentation stands out square from the leaf; the number of bobbins to be left behind, varying according to circumstances; the raised work is usually made with five pair, but for a very tiny jag four pair only will be required. When, however, the points run upwards, as is occasionally the case, the indentations are treated as small leaves, that is, the extra bobbins required

---

* The beautiful dress exhibited by Messrs. Howell and James, at the International Exhibition of 1874, was made in this style, and was, like mine, a reproduction in England of the Belgic lace. This dress was designed by Miss Helen Wilkie, and worked in Devonshire by the most skilled among the Honiton workers.

are added at the tip, and you work back down the point, drawing sewings at one side; to prevent a hole showing where the stem first turns upwards, it is sometimes as well to add an extra pair there to be left behind and worked in at the base; the pinholes should be very close together at this part. There is a form of serrated leaf very common in lace shops, accompanying the nondescript flowers called roses, and as they are also available for small ferns I will give instructions for making them. Carry centre stem to the tip, then work a succession of leaflets down one side as thus:—Work the end one to where it joins the centre fibre, then turn and carry return rope to the place where the points diverge, continue with stem to the tip, and then work back in the usual way, sewing first to the stem, then over the rope, to the base; repeat this for each leaflet. If the lower ones become wider, extra bobbins must be added at their tips, and cut off at the base. When one side is finished, take the bobbins down at the back of the centre stem with return rope, and work the other in the same manner. Having now described all the forms of serrated leaves, I need not give further instructions for them, as the design will show which method is to be pursued. The only failure in the illustration is that the raised stem is not shown with sufficient distinctness, but it should be borne in mind that it will be required at each indentation after the first two or three at the tip. It now remains to describe the different patterns on the leaves, and when that is done you may work the four forming the first scallop without need of further instructions.

CHAPTER XXVI.

Open Dots—Flemish Diamonds—Vandyke Tracing.

The leaves of this design are ornamented in various ways, in order to give it as rich and varied an effect as possible, but the different devices are not essential to the pattern, and those who prefer it may skip this chapter, and work in the usual stitches. It is addressed to those who like diversity, and would rather spend a little more time over their work than continue in one routine.

The fibres I need not describe, they are made as you travel up the centre stem. The open dots are worked either with inner pearl, or in the following manner, which makes a larger hole: Work to the centre, then, instead of sticking a pin for inner pearl, make a turning stitch, and come back to the edge; take up the bobbins on the other side of the hole, work to the opposite edge, and back again to the hole, the last stitch being a turning one; now return to the original bobbins and work across; it will appear at first as if the threads would not draw into their proper places, but they will do so after three or four rows. The small dots arranged in a lozenge-shape are called Flemish diamonds, being merely Flemish dots worked in that form.

All these things are easy, only requiring care and neatness, but a zig-zag device which may be observed on some of the leaves, and which is called Vandyke tracery, is more difficult to master, and must have the closest attention given to it, or it will become a vague and hopeless muddle, and in that case it will be best, if possible, to undo the work, and resort to simple whole-stitch. The vandyke tracery is not marked out with pins, but is formed by twists.

The workers are twisted twice as they pass to and fro, and the passive bobbins on each side of the strand thus formed, only once; the pattern is made by varying the place of the twist. If, for instance, you wish to make a vandyke, and are working across ten pairs of passive bobbins, you will proceed as follows, bearing in mind these two observations, that for the sake of clearness, I do not take into account the outside edge, that being always made as a matter of routine, but I merely reckon across the passive pairs. *i.e.*, those which lie between the pins on each side; also, that when I say twist, I always mean that the workers are to be twisted twice, the passive pairs on each side once.

1st row. Commence from the inner side; work 2 whole stitches, twist, work 8.—2nd row. Work 7, twist, work 3.—3rd row. Work 4, twist, work 6.—4th row. Work 5, twist, work 5.—5th row. work 6, twist, work 4.—6th row. Work 3, twist, work 7.—7th row. Work 8, twist, work 2.

This brings you to the point of the vandyke. 8th row. Work 8, twist, work 7.—9th row. Work 6, twist, work 4.—10th row. Work 5, twist, work 5.—11th row. Work 4, twist, work 6.—12th row. Work 7, twist, work 3. Repeat from 1st row.

You may of course vary the size of the vandyke according to the number of bobbins; but the principle is exactly the same how many soever you work across; if you are adding bobbins on one side, you must keep the count from the other.

You can work a cross by this process on such a space as one of the seed pods; you will have two twists to attend to, as you will commence the two arms of the cross at different sides; bring them down to meet at the middle, then carry them once more to the sides.

I will give directions for a cross over ten pairs of bobbins; of course the size can be altered at pleasure according to the space to be filled. In doing a cross it is always best to put a pin into the middle hole, so as to mark it thoroughly; and in a large space you may twist thrice instead of twice, in order to define it better.

 1st row.—Work 1, twist, work 8, twist, work 1.
 2nd row.—Work 2, twist, work 6, twist, work 2.
 3rd row.—Work 3, twist, work 4, twist, work 3.

4th row.—Work 4, twist, work 2, twist, work 4.
5th row.—Work 5, twist, stick a pin, work 5.
6th row.—Work 4, twist, work 2, twist, work 4.
7th row.—Work 3, twist, work 4, twist, work 3.
8th row.—Work 2, twist, work 6, twist, work 2.
9th row.—Work 1, twist, work 8, twist, work 1.

This sort of tracery looks extremely rich when nicely done; but I end with the remark with which I began, that it requires the closest attention, or it will prove a failure.

CHAPTER XXVII.

Lace in Relief—Flowers—Seed Pods.

In this chapter we come to the most interesting part of the whole book—the lace in relief. We will begin with the flower whose leaves are folding over towards the middle, as that shows the easiest mode of doing it.

I need scarcely say that it is not worked in that shape on the pillow; on the contrary, it is worked quite flat, the centre petals being done first.

FLOWER IN RELIEF.

Work round the inner ring with five pairs, join the circle, add another pair, and work up one side of a petal; add three more pairs, then work in whole stitch, sewing first to the stem, and then to the inner circle, add by degrees four more pairs; you must sew twice, and occasionally three times, into each pin-hole of the centre ring in order to bring the bobbins round; as each petal finishes, cut off, by degrees and very neatly, down to six pair, then work the next one. These petals are not to be joined even where they touch; when the last is finished, and the bobbins cut off to six pair, you will proceed to work the back ones over them in lace stitch.

As a great number of bobbins are required to make these petals full, and as they should look quite even, not crowded in one part and thin in another, you must add the bobbins as you run up the stem, which should be carried about one-third of the way round; each petal will take fifteen or sixteen pair. You will work over the part already done without taking any notice of it, and you can take out the pins that hold it down, as the covering petal will do so; the real difficulty is in the sewings, which are attached to the inner circle like the first ones. The best plan is to sew the small petals to the outer strands of the circle, and the larger ones to the cross strands; three or four sewings will have to be made to the same place in doing the final leaves; when these are completed, put a square plaiting into the centre and out off. Finish off this flower by working the leaf, stem, and seed-pod in the order shewn in the illustration.

Now work the opposite flower, which is done in exactly the same manner, the difference of effect being given afterwards by the needle; one flower appearing to fold over as if half blown, the other opening outwards. A variety is, however, made by the seeds in the middle, this flower being finished off with "crinkle plaitings," but these I shall describe hereafter, as they must be worked on the right side, and are therefore not done till the lace is taken off the pillow. Work the leaf and seed-pod belonging to this second flower, and you may, if you please, put the cross described in the foregoing chapter in the seed-pods, which is worked with thirteen pair.

We now come to the centre flower, which is more difficult to work, inasmuch as it has three tiers of petals; the two first are made in whole, and the back ones in lace, stitch; the edge of the latter must be pearled where it also forms the edge of the scallop. The same directions suffice as for the other flowers, but the difficulty, as before, consists in the sewings, which have to be made to the same places three times over; and it is in these sewings that perfect dexterity and neatness are required, for if you bungle over them you will spoil your work.

Those who cannot master the relief work may work the flowers flat, doing the large petals only, some in whole, and some in lace, stitch to prevent monotony.

There now remain the centre leaves and two seed-pods. Begin with the stem of the drooping one, which starts from the large poppy, and is carried round the curve till it reaches the seed pod. Here you will perceive in the pricking two sets of pinholes in the form of ovals, one being inside the other; this will teach another mode of doing lace in relief. You must work first the large oval, carrying stem all round it; at the base hang on eight more pair, and work whole-stitch to the tip; you may put a cross or lozenge in open tracery if you please, but I would not advise you to do so unless you are tolerably expert at it, as there being sewings on each side, it will not be easy to undo this oval. When you reach the tip, cut off the middle bobbins, leaving five pair on each side, with which make the two points, carrying stem to their tips, and returning to the oval, where sew securely; tie up and cut off. Having now finished the upper part of this seed-pod, take the pins out, and turn it straight back on the pillow with a pin to fasten it down.

Hang on six pair at the base of the small inside oval, sewing to the stem of the upper one, work stem to the tip, hang on seven more pair and a gimp, and work back in whole stitch; this being the foundation oval, the work should be close and firm, fasten once more to the upper stem, tie up and cut off the bobbins. Take out the pins, bring the first oval down into its place, and pin the small one over it; when the ground is put in, it must be sewn to the small oval. Now fasten six pair to the stem, where it intersects the drooping leaf; work stem to the large poppy, come back first with eight

CENTRE FLOWER.

and then with twelve pair where the leaf widens, fastening to the side flower as you pass it; work the second half of the leaf in the same way, cut off.

Do the other leaf, and then the stem of the upright seed-pod. The instructions for this are the same as for the former one, with the exception of the finish, which is made by working stem round the small scallops, and fastening off; this is filled up with crinkle plaitings afterwards, but you may put plain ones if you prefer it. Now ground these flowers and leaves with Devonia ground, which completes this part of the scallop. Here and there you will see a plaiting in the ground, but these I need not particularise.

In any design containing acorns, the cups may be made in the same way as these seed-pods, working the larger portion first, which will stand out in relief on the right side; then turning it back on the pillow, and working the smaller under side over part of the same ground.

CHAPTER XXVIII.

CHEQUER STITCH—LACE IN RELIEF—WORKING OVER STEM.

THE next two scallops are very nearly duplicates of one another; the leaves and flowers, it is true, point in different directions, but the parts which need special instructions are done in the same way, and one description, therefore, will suffice.

For these scallops, you must begin between the two, and work the tendrils, and also the briony berries, before doing the framework leaves. The tendrils are simply worked in stem-stitch, each commencing at the point of one of the side leaves, and ending on itself. The berries are done in a new stitch, called chequer stitch, which I will here describe: Begin at the base of one of the lower berries, work stem all round : leave the three outer pairs to carry on the stem afterwards; hang on six more pairs. You will have (there being stem on both sides) one pair of workers, which will pass backwards and forwards across eight pair; be careful that there are no knots in this working pair.

Chequer stitch is done in this manner: Work one, twist the workers thrice, work two, twist thrice, work two, twist thrice, work one, and sew to the stem. Repeat this row three times, then sew the workers to the next pin hole, twist all the passive pairs three times, and repeat the three rows; then once more sew to two pin holes in succession, and twist the passive pairs. Chequer stitch is very easy and makes a good variation; the only thing to be careful about is to draw each twist well up.

Cut off at the end of the berry, return to the stem, fasten on three pairs, work the tendril and stem to the middle berry, which is done as the other, the only difference being that you do not leave three pairs behind this time, but hang on three after working stem all round, fill with chequer stitch, cut off three at the end, and proceed to the next berry. Now do the leaves forming the frame-work, for which I need not give directions, there being only one thing to notice, and that is that one point of the leaf turns up, this, however, is done afterwards; you must work up the leaf as if it were not there.

Again we must return to the lace in relief, of which this scallop shows different specimens, some of which are difficult, and require careful working. Wherever this raised part is smaller than the background, it is plain sailing enough; you work the raised petals, and do the larger ones over them. With the seed-pods the case is reversed, the relief part being larger than the foundation, but as they start from a stem, they are easily turned back, and the small portion worked over the same ground. In the side-long

POPPY AND BRIONY DESIGN. No. 2. (Page 72.)

CHEQUER STITCH—LACE IN RELIEF—WORKING OVER STEM.

flowers, and butterflies with their wings folded, the two sides are equal in size, nevertheless, they may be turned back like the seed-pods, and the second, or under side worked into the same holes; but this is not practicable where, as in the case of the half closed briony leaves, there is a length of mutual foundation, here the two parts must be worked exactly over one another, and into the same pin-holes.

The butterflies must be done first, so as to complete the edge of the scallops, work the body with seven pair, then with five pair do the tracery inside the wings, now carry stem all round the foremost wing, doing the outside edge first; and as you pass up it, hang on a pair at each pin-hole except the three corner ones, which must each have two pairs; those extra bobbins I need not say are to be left behind to be ready for the lace stitch with which you will fill up the wing as soon as you arrive at the base, fasten the tracery with a sewing as you pass over it. You may pearl the edge of this wing or not as you please, the foundation wing *must* be pearled, as it forms the edge of the lace; it looks better to have both wings the same, but the sewings are more difficult, therefore I leave it to the discretion of each individual worker. In working this wing, you must contrive so as to end at the further corner: cut off to five pairs, and work stem round the other wing to the base, hanging on the extra pairs at each of the three corner holes, and one at the remaining holes; fill with lace stitch, and cut off. Now turn the wing completely back, fold a piece of tissue paper, and pin it down over it. Hang on five pair to the body, and work the wings precisely as before, but fastening them to the framework leaves on each side. It is obvious that these wings cannot be worked over one another, the inner tracery forbids it, the first made would be hopelessly spoiled, however careful the working.

Now work the half briony leaf, and the tendril, then the plain seed pod; bring the stem of the latter to the leaf, turn and work buckle stitch to the side-long flower. In doing this you have to pass over several stems and a leaf; it is easy to pass simple stem across another portion of lace, as you may plait the threads, but this you cannot do with buckle stitch. You must therefore have a small piece of passement pricked for this stem as far as you require it; fold tissue paper over the lace, pin down the small pricking with a pad of cotton wool between it and the paper, and carry your stem over this little bridge; you must put your pins in carefully, and very slanting, as they must not run through the tissue paper, remove the extra passement and cotton wool as soon as you have passed over the lace.

The side-long flowers are now to be done; they are slightly different, as the one seems scarcely open, whereas the petals of the other are more expanding, and curve outwards; they are made with the same number of bobbins, but the petals are joined together in one, and made separate in the other. The first set of petals are worked in whole-stitch, both the side ones being finished before the middle one is done; the side petals will take about ten pairs, the middle one seventeen, the bulk of which must be hung on as you work stem up the side; the finish will be at the further corner, in the flower whose petals are joined; in the other stem must be carried further round, and you will end at the base. Turn back the lace over its stem, protecting it with tissue paper, work the under petals in lace stitch, and these are to be joined together in both cases. Now work the little point of the leaf which turns up, and this is done with a separate pricking, and a pad of cotton wool as in the stem, hang on eight pairs at the tip, work to the leaf, sew two or three pairs to a pin hole, cut off neatly, and turn the point under.

CHAPTER XXIX.

Side Leaves—Antwerp Diamonds—Wheels.

THE only remaining description of lace in relief to be given, is the side briony leaf. Begin at the end of the tendril, follow it to the leaf, there continue the stem up the back, but not as for raised work, as the leaf curves the wrong way. Hang on two pair at the tip, and work back in whole stitch, sewing to the outside strands of the stem, or centre fibre; when you come to the first division of the leaf, carry raised work to the tip, hanging on two extra pairs at the first hole, and one at each of the succeeding holes; work straight back from the tip to the centre fibre; you must sew twice into each hole, and occasionally thrice, as there are so many more outside than inside holes. The next point is done by spreading the bobbins, and following the course of the outside holes; when you reach the tip and are coming down the last edge, gather the five pairs next to the pins in a cluster, which pass between the workers in one row, and under them in the next in the same way that you treat a gimp. You must arrange your sewings so as to finish this side of the leaf neatly at the base. Now turn your pillow without cutting off any of the bobbins, and work back over the same ground, but the reverse way: it has a better effect of light and shade, if this half is done in lace-stitch; but as this leaf is rather puzzling, the first one you do had better be in whole stitch. The sewings to the centre fibre must now be made to the cross strands, and two or three to one place as before; the outside edge is worked into the same holes as the first half, but as there must be no raised work up the point for fear of joining the two sides together in drawing the sewings, you must expand or compress your work, as the course of the holes suggests, and you must skip one here and there

SIDE LEAVES—ANTWERP DIAMONDS—WHEELS.

when they are close together in order to keep the outside and inside level with each other. Bring a cluster of five pair down the side of the last point: out off to eight pair, work to the tip; tie up the bobbins, but do not cut them off, as they will work into the ground: you must be very careful in sewing the ground to this leaf, to fasten it to the part last worked, and not to the lace that lies below it.

Now, work the centre leaves and the drooping bud; which latter is simply made by working the oval calyx first, and doing the flower, which appears as if it were just bursting open, over it in lace stitch.

When the inside of the scallops are finished and grounded, the border is next to be worked, and that contains two novelties, the Wheel, and Antwerp Diamond stitch. The latter is little more than chequer stitch worked slantwise, so that the divisions come in diamonds instead of squares; it is done in the following way: hang on eleven pairs at the tip of one of the border leaves; you will have three working pairs, one passive pair on each side next the pins, and six other pairs which will be arranged in sets of three; work from the outside across the passive pair next the pins (which is called the side pair) twist the workers thrice, work three stitches, the last being a turning stitch; come back to the edge again, twisting the workers before doing the side pair. In the third row you work the side pair, twist, work two, the last a turning stitch; return to the edge as before. For the fifth row you work the side pair, twist, make a turning stitch, return; then work the side pair only and back again, this will bring the workers down another hole, and is equivalent to making the two sewings together, as you did in chequer stitch. Twist all the passive pairs, (except the two side ones, which are never to be twisted) four or five times. You have now made the preliminary diamond, and have got your work in a slant; from this time you work as follows: work 1, twist, work 3, twist, work 3, twist, work 1; repeat this row three times, then, whichever side you are at, work over the side pair and back again, twist the six middle pairs, and work three rows, again twisting after the 1st, 4th, and 7th stitches. You will of course end on one side sooner than the other, but you will wind up as you began, working across four and back, then across three, and then two.

When this leaf is finished out off to six pair, work the circle and the other leaf, which is merely raised work and lace stitch.

The Wheel is next to be done, which completes the border pattern. Here I must ask for your closest attention, especially for the work in the middle, which will appear involved, and difficult to understand, until the plan on which it is done is thoroughly learned by heart. Work round the edge with six pair in stem-stitch, join the circle and cut off to two pair; bring these inside and sew to the nearest hole; make a plait to the centre, stick a pin between the pairs, twist both twice; hang on two pair at the neighbouring hole, plait to the centre, stick a pin, twist the strands, and make a stitch with pairs 2 and 3, which lie between the two pins; twist the strands again, in fact this is to be done after every stitch. Bring the third plait to the centre, stick a pin, twist, and make a stitch with pairs 4 and 5; bring the fourth plait down in like manner, and make a stitch with 6 and 7. You have now got all the bobbins into the middle of the wheel with all the strands twisted. For the first row, make a stitch with 8 and 7, put aside 8, sticking a pin by it, then with 6 and 5, with 4 and 3, 2 and 1, twisting always; put aside 1, sticking a pin by it. In the second row you make stitches between 2 and 3, 4 and 5, 6 and 7; in the third row between 6 and 5, and 4 and 3, putting aside the end pair on each side, and sticking a pin; finally make a stitch between 4 and 5. You have now all your bobbins arranged for the remaining plaits: make them to the edge, sew, tie up, and cut off.

You will probably have to work this wheel two or three times before you thoroughly understand the principle on which it is done. It is that the threads are not taken straight across, but you work in detached stitches on neighbouring pairs, the relative positions of which change in each row, so that the strands come across each other in a sort of open work.

CHAPTER XXX.

Italian Ground—Butterfly—Crinkle Plaitings—Setting Up Devonia Lace.

Having finished the length of Border, the grounding between the scallops has to be filled in: this ground you will observe is composed of sexagons; having all the sides equal.

It was used for grounding the old Italian coarse laces; but there is a slight difference in the stitch: I will teach the real stitch afterwards, but the Honiton thread is too fine for it in sexagons of this size. Begin at the left hand side of the place to be filled, say, immediately under one of the wheels, to which fasten four pairs, and work a plait right and left as far as the two holes below; stick a pin temporarily to hold the bobbins; fasten on four more at the tip of a leaf, and plait right and left as before. The right hand plait first made will meet the left-hand one of the second set; you must now deal with the bobbins in pairs instead of single threads; take out the pin you put in to hold the threads, pass the middle left hand pair over the middle right, stick in the pin again between them; twist each pair to a fine strand, and with these four strands make a plait down the straight side of the sexagon, stick a pin in the hole at the bottom, untwist the threads, and make a plait right and left as before. Return to the border, fasten on four more pairs, and bring a fresh line of plaits down in the same manner;

if you twist your strands firmly there will be no perceptible difference in the size of the plaits. As it is difficult to manage knots in this ground, you had better wind them well away before beginning, but should one unfortunately appear, you must deal with it at the commencement of the strand plait.

The old stitch being, as I before observed, done with coarse thread, is a little different; the stitch is as follows: Put the middle left hand bobbin over the middle right, give both pairs one twist to the left; repeat. When the right and left lines meet, twist the strands, put the middle left strand over the middle right, stick a pin to hold them, then work with the twisted strands in the same stitch as before.

You may vary this ground by putting a pearl irregularly here and there, about halfway down the plait on either side, but it should not be on the strand plait. Of course this stitch may be done with Honiton thread, but the hexagon must be a great deal smaller and closer; it will give very much the effect of a Valenciennes ground.

The only part of the design still undescribed is the butterfly, with its wings expanded; but as the Italian ground cannot be well worked over it, this is made separately, and fastened on afterwards. Begin at the body, then do the inner tracery, and next the raised work round the wings, hanging on extra bobbins for filling in the lace-stitch background in the same way as directed for the other butterflies. You need not make all these butterflies the same, in fact it would be an improvement in a length of lace to vary them as much as possible, working some of their wings in chequer stitch or Antwerp diamonds, and others with the large holes described in a previous chapter.

When the full length of the design is finished, take it off the pillow, and work another. You may, if you please, join the lengths as you go by pinning down the finished piece, and sewing the new one at the points of contact; but as it is not easy to keep the lace clean and uncrumpled, it is much better to work the lengths separate, and join them afterwards over blue paper; you must in this case have an extra pricking of one of the triangular pieces of the Italian ground, and fill this portion in at the time of joining.

The interiors of the poppies have also to be filled in on the right side with the crinkle plaitings: these are only long plaits, which when completed, are fastened back either with a sewing or a stitch very nearly as far as the place they started from; so that they stand up in loops, and afford a very fair representation of stamens.

The lace being finished and taken off the pillow, it must now go through the process of "setting up," which is a very dainty and delicate part of the work: while you are about it, let the lace lie loosely on tissue paper, or a clean handkerchief; it should not be folded up, or have a weight placed upon it. Before you begin to work, wash your hands in warm water; it is better to make this an invariable rule, as of necessity you must handle the lace a good deal, and though it can be cleaned, yet it never looks so well afterwards, as indeed no lace really does. Take the finest possible needle, and with lace thread adjust the petals in their places: to fasten off it will be sufficient to make a stitch, and pass the needle once through the loop, draw it up, and cut off the thread quite close; you may have a little knot at the end of your thread when you begin, if you run it under one of the raised stems it will not show.

The first poppy which folds over towards the middle, has simply a thread run along the edge of the minor petals; you may draw them close, or leave them partly open according to fancy: the opposite one curves its leaves back, and these you arrange by fastening them down lightly to the back petals, some with one stitch, others with two, running the thread at the back of the lace; don ot try to do them regularly, the greater variety you can give, the more artistic the effect. The middle poppy will require both modes of treatment, the inner petals being disposed to stand up, the middle ones curved downwards. For the one side long flower, you merely have to sew both sides together; the other, which is more open, should not be sewn all the way, and the middle petal is caught to the side ones, for the space of three or four holes from the bottom. The seed pods require neat and careful work; the large oval has to be sewn to the small one on both sides, but not at the tip; this rounds it, and causes it to stand out boldly. Fasten down the calyx of the opening flower with a stitch at the tip; and lastly sew on the loose butterflies, which you may place in different attitudes according to your own liking.

Having done all this, the finishing touch must be put as follows: Boil a quarter of an ounce of rice in about a pint of water, so as to get the very thinnest possible starch, to give a *soupçon* merely of stiffness; when cold strain it off, and with a camel's hair pencil brush over the inside of the parts standing out in relief. They should be merely damped, not made very wet. Where you wish to get a bold curve, as in the sidelong flower which turns its petals outwards, use an ivory knitting needle dipped in the ricewater to mould it over: this also may be inserted into the seed pods, if the space at the tip is sufficiently open. In fact wherever a rounded appearance is required, the knitting needle is more useful than the brush; but the latter is best for the half leaves, and the butterflies' wings, also in several places where the needle cannot be inserted without risk of tearing out the stitches.

The Devonia kind of lace does not fold over well, as may readily be apprehended; sharp corners are therefore to be avoided in trimming dresses with it, though it may be arranged round curves. For such a piece of lace as would be required for a square or V shaped bodice for instance, the design should be specially drawn for the corners; and it would be best to mount the lace on ribbon, as it can be at once placed on the dress, without all the fingering which it must otherwise undergo, and which might crush the petals.

Groups of flowers look extremely well in this species of lace appliquéd on velvet, satin, or silk; they make exquisite banner screens; or may be let in as centre panels to small table cabinets; but in this case they should either be behind glass, or have a cover to save them from dust. These groups are not grounded, but the appliqué work must be done in a frame.

"Devonia's" work is now done: the labour is ended which, slight and unimportant as it may appear, has yet had power to beguile many a sad and weary hour of a chequered life. She cannot close without an expression of gratitude to her numerous and most kind correspondents, who, though strangers, have seemed to her as friends; and to whom she wishes all success in the interesting and beautiful art in which she has had the pleasure of instructing them.

INDEX.

A.

Acorns in relief . . . . *page*	71
Adding bobbins	18
at tip of leaf	26
passing up stem	38
ditto for petals	61
Antwerp diamonds	75

B.

Bead edge	36
Beginner's stem	12
Bobbins	8
bag	8
to cut off	34
to wind	9
Border Scallop	48
Shamrock	36
Trefoil	25
Wheel and Diamond . . .	75
Wild Rose	32
Wood Sorrel	33
Braid buckle	61
Cucumber	35
open	35
open bead	43
plain	35
Butterfly, Emperor	57
half	38
in relief	73
Peacock	31

C.

Camellia spray	50
Centre fibre	41
Chequer stitch	72
Convolvulus spray	61

Cover cloths . . . . . *page*	8
Crinkle plaitings	77
Cucumber braid	35
Plaitings	32

D.

Dame Joan Ground	53
Devonia Ground	48
lace in relief	69
acorns and seed pods . . .	71
butterflies	73
leaves	74
spray	23

E.

Edge, pearl, left	31
pearl, right	25
plain	10

F.

False pin holes	18
Fern spray	56
leaflets	67
Fibre branching	49
centre	42
stitch	22
Finish of leaf	21
Footings	35, 43

G.

Gimp	8
to work	14

INDEX

Grounds, needle:
- Dame Joan . . . page 53
- Net . . . 43
- Star . . . 52
- Strand . . . 34

Grounds, pillow:
- Devonia . . . 48
- Honiton . . . 42
- Italian . . . 76
- Net . . . 43

H.

- Half hitch . . . 9
- Headings . . . 35
- Hook . . . 8

I.

- Inner pearl . . . 38
- Ivy leaf pattern . . . 42

K.

- Knots . . . 12
- in lace stitch . . . 17

L.

- Lace stitch . . . 16
- Leaves to finish . . . 21
  - with raised work . . . 26
  - to work in halves . . . 33
  - another method . . . 37
  - with centre fibre . . . 41
  - open branching fibres . . . 42
  - close ditto . . . 49
  - in relief . . . 74
  - serrated . . . 66
- Lime Blossom . . . 38

N.

- Needle pin . . . 8
  - mode of using . . . 27

O.

- Open braid . . . 35
  - dots . . . 67
  - fibres . . . 42
  - trefoil . . . 15

P.

- Passement . . . page 8
- Passing over work . . . 73
- Patterns, Camellia . . . 50
  - Convolvulus . . . 61
  - Daisy . . . 28
  - Daisy collar . . . 41
  - Fern . . . 56
  - Half butterfly . . . 38
  - Ivy leaf . . . 43
  - Lily lappet . . . 46
  - Lime blossom . . . 38
  - Peacock Butterfly . . . 31
  - Poppy and Briony . . . 65
  - Shamrock . . . 36
  - Trefoil edging . . . 25
  - Wild Rose . . . 37
  - Wood Sorrel . . . 33
- Pearl, left . . . 31
  - right . . . 25
  - inner . . . 38
- Pillow . . . 8
- Pins . . . 8
- Pincushion . . . 8
- Pistile . . . 26
- Plaitings, crinkle . . . 77
  - Cucumber . . . 82
  - long or diamond . . . 29
  - square . . . 50

R.

- Raised work . . . 26
- Relief work, Acorns . . . 71
  - Butterflies . . . 73
  - Flowers . . . 69
  - Leaves . . . 74
  - Seed pods . . . 70
- Reverse folds to leaves . . . 47
- Rope . . . 27
  - return . . . 41

S.

- Scissors, cutting off . . . 84
- Seed pods, in relief . . . 70
- Serrated leaves . . . 66
  - another method . . . 67
- Setting up Devonia lace . . . 78
- Sewing with hook . . . 15, 20
  - with middle pin . . . 27
- Sewing centre fibre . . . 41
  - rope . . . 27
- Shifting lace on pillow . . . 25
- Square plaitings . . . 50

INDEX.

Stem, beginner's . . . . page	12
Buckle	61
ordinary	14
Starch	78
Stitch, Antwerp Diamond . .	75
Chequer	72
Dame Joan	53
Flemish	62
Flemish diamond	63
Fibre	22
Lace	16
Net needle	42
Net pillow	42
Open dots	67
Star	52
Vandyke tracing	68
Wheel	73
Whole	10

T.

Thread 8
Tracing 57
   vandyke 68
   cross 68

Trefoil, open . . . . . page 14
   close 18
   pearl edge 25
Turning scallops 28
Twists 19
Tying up bobbins 12

U.

Unwinding bobbins 19

V.

Vandyke tracery 68

W.

Wheels 75
Wild Rose border 37
Winding bobbins 9
Winding up 19
Wood Sorrel border 33

ERRATUM.

₊ I find I am in error in saying that Messrs. Howell and James's dress was a reproduction from the Belgic; the details of the raised flowers, &c., were copied from a piece of old Roman lace. I myself took the idea of the relief work from a Belgian flounce, which I once saw casually in passing, and which had here and there raised petals to the flowers. Olive and I, and an ingenious and appreciative lace maker, Mrs. Carter, of Exmouth, carried out further details, and perfected the process between us.   DEVONIA.

PRICE LIST.

The charges for the pricked patterns have been further reduced, as I have made a fresh arrangement respecting them.

The bobbins, which I now have made only of boxwood, are rather dearer, and there is in consequence a slight increase in the price of the lace pillows.

PRICKED PATTERNS.

	s.	d.
Length of Poppy and Briony	6	0
Ivy Leaf	4	6
Convolvulus Head dress	2	6
Daisy Collar	2	0
Lily Lappet	2	0
Fern and Camellia spray, each	1	0
Trefoil, Wild Rose, and Wood Sorrel Borders, each	0	8
Emperor and Peacock Buttterflies, each	0	6
Shamrock Border	0	6
Daisy and Devonia sprays, each	0	3
Braids, 6, 1in. lengths, each	0	3
Small sprays, each	0	1
Pillows, fitted up	16	0
Bobbins, boxwood, per dozen	0	9
Thread, per hank	0	7
Gimp, per hank	0	3
Pins, per paper	0	6½
Sewing Hooks, each	0	5
Sheet of Passement	0	6

All orders should be accompanied by stamps, or P. O. Orders payable to L. UPCOTT. P. O. Orders must be payable at King-street, Covent-garden. Orders will be executed in rotation, and as speedily as possible.

DEVONIA.

*** Letters and orders should be addressed "Devonia," care of Manager of *The Bazaar*, 170, Strand, W.C.

KNITTING SILK.

IMPERIAL AND ROYAL,
Any colour, 1s. 6d. per oz.

IMPERIAL AND ROYAL TUSSORE,
Undyed, 1s. 3d. per oz.

The above silks are kept in two sizes. The quantity required is 2oz. for socks, and 4oz. for a pair of very long stockings.

FILOSELLE.

2s. per oz. of 8 skeins (all one shade); 2s. 6d. per oz. of 8 skeins (mixed shades), or per single skein, 4d.

EMBROIDERY SILK.

An oz. hank, or 14 skeins of 20yds. each (all one shade) 1s. 6d.; 1oz. of 14 skeins (mixed shades) 2s., or per single skein, 2d.

SHADED EMBROIDERY SILK,
6d. per oz. extra, or per single skein, 3d.

CHURCH EMBROIDERY,
4s. per oz.

ORDERS DESPATCHED BY RETURN OF POST TO ALL PARTS OF THE UNITED KINGDOM.

Patterns Free.

ADAMS AND CO.,
MANUFACTURERS,
5, New Street, Bishopsgate Street, London, E.

(DISCOUNT TO THE TRADE.)

ADVERTISEMENTS.

USEFUL BOOKS.

RABBITS for PRIZES and PROFIT. By CHARLES RAYSON. Contains, Hutches, Breeding, Feeding, Diseases and their Treatment, Rabbits as a Food Supply, and careful descriptions of Angora, Belgian Hare, Dutch, Himalayan, Lop, Patagonian, Siberian, Silver Grey, and Polish Fancy Rabbits, with full page portraits of prize specimens. Large post 8vo., price 2s. 6d.
"General Management" and "Exhibition Rabbits" may be had separately, price 1s. each.

POULTRY for PRIZES and PROFIT. By JAMES LONG. Profusely Illustrated. In parts, large post 8vo., price 6d. each.
I.—BREEDING POULTRY FOR PRIZES.—Fourth Edition.
II.—EXHIBITION POULTRY (Part I.).—Third Edition.
III.—EXHIBITION POULTRY (Part II.).—Second Edition.
IV.—MANAGEMENT of the POULTRY YARD.—Second Edition.

THE BOOK of the GOAT: containing Practical Directions for the Management of the Milch Goat in Health and Disease. Illustrated. By STEPHEN HOLMES. Cloth gilt, price 2s. 6d., by post 2s. 8d.

THE DISEASES OF DOGS: their Pathology, Diagnosis, and Treatment. To which is added a complete Dictionary of Canine Materia Medica. By HUGH DALZIEL. Large post 8vo., in paper price 1s., in cloth gilt 2s.

BREAKING and TRAINING DOGS: being concise directions for the proper Education both for Field and for Companions, of Retrievers, Pointers, Setters, Spaniels, Terriers, &c. By "PATHFINDER" (of "The Country," &c.). Large post 8vo. In cloth gilt, 5s.; by post 5s. 4d.

TURNING for AMATEURS, containing full description of the lathe, with all its working parts and attachments, and minute instructions for the effective use of them on wood, metal, and ivory. Illustrated with 130 first-class wood engravings. SECOND EDITION. Large post 8vo., cloth, price 2s. 6d.

WORKING IN SHEET METAL: being practical instruction for making and mending small Articles in Tin, Copper, Iron, Zinc, and Brass. Illustrated. SECOND EDITION. Large post 8vo., price 6d.

CARPENTRY and JOINERY for AMATEURS. Contains full descriptions of the various Tools required in the above Arts, together with practical instructions for their use. By the Author of "Turning for Amateurs," "Working in Sheet Metal," &c. Large post 8vo. In Monthly Parts, price 6d.; by post 6½d.

WOOD CARVING for AMATEURS: containing descriptions of all the requisite Tools, and full instructions for their use in producing different varieties of Carvings. Illustrated. Large post 8vo., price 1s., by post 1s. 1d.

BRITISH MARINE ALGÆ: Being a Popular Account of the SEAWEEDS of GREAT BRITAIN, their Collection and Preservation. By W. H. GRATTANN. Magnificently Illustrated with 205 engravings. Large post 8vo., price 5s. 6d., by post 5s. 10d.

THE ART of PYROTECHNY: Being Comprehensive and Practical Instructions for the MANUFACTURE of FIREWORKS, specially designed for the use of Amateurs. Profusely Illustrated. By W. H. BROWNE, Ph.D., M.A., L.R.C.P., &c. Large post 8vo., price 3s. 6d.

Catalogue of Practical Handbooks Published by L. Upcott Gill, 170, Strand, London, W.C.

ANGLER, BOOK OF THE ALL-ROUND. A Comprehensive Treatise on Angling in both Fresh and Salt Water. In Four Divisions: 1, Coarse Fish; 2, Pike; 3, Game Fish; 4, Sea Fish. Each Division is complete in itself, as named below. By JOHN BICKERDYKE. With over 220 Engravings. *In cloth, price 5s. 6d.* LARGE PAPER EDITION (200 copies only, signed and numbered), *bound in Roxburghe, price 21s. to Subscribers.*

    Angling for Coarse Fish. A very Complete and Practical Work on Bottom Fishing, according to the methods in use on the Thames, Trent, Norfolk Broads, and elsewhere. Illustrated. *Price 1s., cloth 2s. (uncut).*

    Angling for Pike. A Practical and Comprehensive Work on the most Approved Methods of Fishing for Pike or Jack; including an Account of Some New Tackles for Spinning, Live-baiting, and Trolling. Profusely Illustrated. *Price 1s., cloth 2s. (uncut).*

    Angling for Game Fish. A Practical Treatise on the Various Methods of Fishing for Salmon; Moorland, Chalk-stream, and Thames Trout; Grayling, and Char. Well Illustrated. *Price 1s. 6d., cloth 2s. 6d. (uncut).*

    Angling in Salt Water. A Practical Work on Sea Fishing with Rod and Line, from the Shore, Piers, Jetties, Rocks, and from Boats; together with Some Account of Hand-Lining. Over 50 Engravings. *Price 1s., cloth 2s. (uncut).*

BEE-KEEPING, BOOK OF. A very Practical and Complete Manual on the Proper Management of Bees, especially written for Beginners and Amateurs who have but a few Hives. Fully Illustrated. By W. B. WEBSTER, First-class Expert, B.B.K.A. *Price 1s.; in cloth, 1s. 6d.*

BEES AND BEE-KEEPING: Scientific and Practical. By F. R. CHESHIRE, F.L.S., F.R.M.S., Lecturer on Apiculture at South Kensington. *In two vols., price 16s.*

    Vol. I., Scientific. A complete Treatise on the Anatomy and Physiology of the Hive Bee. *In cloth gilt, price 7s. 6d.*

    Vol. II., Practical Management of Bees. An Exhaustive Treatise on Advanced Bee Culture. *In cloth gilt, price 8s. 6d.*

BICYCLES AND TRICYCLES OF THE YEAR. Descriptions of the New Inventions and Improvements for the Present Season. Designed to assist intending purchasers in the choice of a machine. Illustrated. By HARRY HEWITT GRIFFIN. (Published Annually.) *In paper, price 1s.*

BOAT BUILDING AND SAILING, PRACTICAL. Containing Full Instructions for Designing and Building Punts, Skiffs, Canoes, Sailing Boats, &c. Particulars of the most Suitable Sailing Boats and Yachts for Amateurs, and Instructions for their Proper Handling. Fully Illustrated with Designs and Working Diagrams. By ADRIAN NEISON, C.E., DIXON KEMP, A.I.N.A., and G. CHRISTOPHER DAVIES. *In one vol., cloth gilt, price 7s. 6d.*

BOAT BUILDING FOR AMATEURS, PRACTICAL. Containing Full Instructions for Designing and Building Punts, Skiffs, Canoes, Sailing Boats, &c. Fully Illustrated with Working Diagrams. By ADRIAN NEISON, C.E. Second Edition, Revised and Enlarged by DIXON KEMP, Author of "Yacht Designing," "A Manual of Yacht and Boat Sailing," &c. *In cloth gilt, price 2s. 6d.*

BOAT SAILING FOR AMATEURS. Containing Particulars of the most Suitable Sailing Boats and Yachts for Amateurs, and Instructions for their Proper Handling, &c. Illustrated with numerous Diagrams. By G. CHRISTOPHER DAVIES. Second Edition, Revised and Enlarged, and with several New Plans of Yachts. *In cloth gilt, price 5s.*

BOOKBINDING FOR AMATEURS: Being Descriptions of the various Tools and Appliances Required, and Minute Instructions for their Effective Use. By W. J. E. CRANE. Illustrated with 156 Engravings. *In cloth gilt, price 2s. 6d.*

BROADS, THE LAND OF THE. By E. R. SUFFLING.

ILLUSTRATED EDITION.—The most Complete Guide to the whole of the District—embracing the Broads and their Waterways of Norfolk and Suffolk—that has yet been published. A good Map of the Broads, Rivers, Chief Roads, and Places named, *printed in four* colours, accompanies the work. *Price 2s. 6d.*

CHEAP EDITION.—An abridged Edition of the above, with some Plates of Characteristic Sketches by J. TEMPLE. A good and *clear* Map, in black and white, is also given. In Coloured Cover, *price 1s.*

BUTTERFLIES AND MOTHS, COLLECTING: Being Directions for Capturing, Killing, and Preserving Lepidoptera and their Larvæ. Illustrated. Reprinted, with Additions, from "Practical Taxidermy." By MONTAGU BROWNE. *In paper, price 1s.*

CACTUS CULTURE FOR AMATEURS: Being Descriptions of the various Cactuses grown in this country; with Full and Practical Instructions for their Successful Cultivation. By W. WATSON, Assistant Curator of the Royal Botanic Gardens, Kew. Profusely Illustrated. *In cloth gilt, price 5s.*

CAGE BIRDS, BRITISH. Containing Full Directions for Successfully Breeding, Rearing, and Managing the various British Birds that can be kept in Confinement. Illustrated with COLOURED PLATES and numerous finely cut Wood Engravings. By R. L. WALLACE. *In cloth gilt, price 10s. 6d.*

❖ **All Books Post Free.**

CAGE BIRDS, DISEASES OF: Their Cause, Symptoms, and Treatment. A Handbook which should be in the hands of everyone who keeps a Bird. By Dr. W. T. GREENE, F.Z.S. *In paper, price* 1s.

CANARY BOOK. Containing Full Directions for the Breeding, Rearing, and Management of all Varieties of Canaries and Canary Mules, the Promotion and Management of Canary Societies and Exhibitions, and all other matters connected with this Fancy. By ROBERT L. WALLACE. Second Edition, Enlarged and Revised, with many new Illustrations of Prize Birds, Cages, &c. *In cloth gilt, price* 5s.*; Coloured Plates*, 6s. 6d.*;* and in Sections as follows :

Canaries, General Management of. Including Cages and Cage-making, Breeding, Managing, Mule Breeding, Diseases and their Treatment, Moulting, Rats and Mice, &c. Illustrated. *In cloth, price* 2s. 6d.

Canaries, Exhibition. Containing Full Particulars of all the different Varieties, their Points of Excellence, Preparing Birds for Exhibition, Formation and Management of Canary Societies and Exhibitions. Illustrated. *In cloth, price* 2s. 6d.

CARD TRICKS, BOOK OF, for Drawing-room and Stage Entertainments by Amateurs ; with an Exposure of Tricks as practised by Card Sharpers and Swindlers. Numerous Illustrations. By Prof. R. KUNARD. *Illustrated Wrapper, price* 2s. 6d.

CHURCH EMBROIDERY: Its Early History and Manner of Working ; Materials Used and Stitches Employed ; Raised and Flat Couching, Appliqué, &c., &c., including Church Work over Cardboard. A practical handbook for Church Workers. Illustrated. *In paper, price* 1s.

CHURCH FESTIVAL DECORATIONS. Comprising Directions and Designs for the Suitable Decoration of Churches for Christmas, Easter, Whitsuntide, and Harvest. Illustrated. A useful book for the Clergy and their Lay Assistants. *In paper, price* 1s.

COFFEE STALL MANAGEMENT, PRACTICAL HINTS ON, and other Temperance Work for the Laity. *In paper, price* 1s.

COINS, A GUIDE TO ENGLISH PATTERN, in Gold, Silver, Copper, and Pewter, from Edward I. to Victoria, with their Value. By the REV. G. F. CROWTHER, M.A. Illustrated. *In silver cloth, with gilt facsimiles of Coins, price* 5s.

COINS OF GREAT BRITAIN AND IRELAND, A GUIDE TO THE, in Gold, Silver, and Copper, from the Earliest Period to the Present Time, with their Value. By the late Colonel W. STEWART THORBURN. Of immense value to collectors and dealers. 27 Plates in Gold, Silver, and Copper, and 8 Plates of Gold and Silver Coins in RAISED FACSIMILE. *In cloth, with silver facsimiles of Coins, price* 7s. 6d.

COLLIE, THE. Its History, Points, and Breeding. By HUGH DALZIEL. Illustrated. *Demy 8vo, price 1s.; cloth, 2s.*

COLUMBARIUM, MOORE'S. Reprinted Verbatim from the original Edition of 1735, with a Brief Notice of the Author. By W. B. TEGETMEIER, F.Z.S. *Price 1s.*

COOKERY FOR AMATEURS; or, French Dishes for English Homes of all Classes. Includes Simple Cookery, Middle-class Cookery, Superior Cookery, Cookery for Invalids, and Breakfast and Luncheon Cookery. By MADAME VALÉRIE. Second Edition. *In paper, price 1s.*

CUCUMBER CULTURE FOR AMATEURS. Including also Melons, Vegetable Marrows, and Gourds. Illustrated. By W. J. MAY. *In paper, price 1s.*

DEGREES, A GUIDE TO, in Arts, Science, Literature, Law, Music, and Divinity, in the United Kingdom, the Colonies, the Continent, and the United States. By E. WOOTON, Author of "A Guide to the Medical Profession," &c. *In cloth, price 15s.*

DOGS, BREAKING AND TRAINING: Being Concise Directions for the proper Education of Dogs, both for the Field and for Companions. Second Edition. By "PATHFINDER." With Chapters by HUGH DALZIEL on Work of Special Breeds; Trail or Drag Hounds; Training Bloodhounds; Defenders and Watch Dogs; Sheep Dogs—Stock Tenders; Life Savers—Water Dogs; Vermin Destroyers; House Manners; Behaviour Out of Doors. Illustrated. *In cloth gilt, price 6s. 6d.*

DOGS, BRITISH : Their Varieties, History, and Characteristics. By HUGH DALZIEL, assisted by Eminent Fanciers. NEW EDITION, Revised and Enlarged. Illustrated with First-class COLOURED PLATES and full-page Engravings of Dogs of the Day. This will be the fullest and most recent work on the various breeds of dogs kept in England, and, as its Author is one of the first living authorities on the subject, its accuracy can be relied upon. Demy 8vo. In two Volumes, *price 10s. 6d.* each, as follows :

Dogs Used in Field Sports. Containing Particulars of the following, among other Breeds: Greyhound, Irish Wolfhound, Bloodhound, Foxhound, Harrier, Basset, Dachshund, Pointer, Setters, Spaniels, and Retrievers. SEVEN COLOURED PLATES and 21 full-page Engravings. *In cloth gilt, price 10s. 6d.*

Dogs Useful to Man in other Work than Field Sports; House and Toy Dogs. Containing Particulars of the following, among other Breeds : Collie, Bulldog, Mastiff, St. Bernard, Newfoundland, Great Dane, Fox and all other Terriers, King Charles and Blenheim Spaniels, Pug, Pomeranian, Poodle, Italian Greyhound, Toy Dogs, &c., &c. Coloured Plates and full-page Engravings. *In cloth gilt, price 10s. 6d.*

❖ **All Books Post Free.**

DOGS, DISEASES OF: Their Causes, Symptoms, and Treatment; Modes of Administering Medicines; Treatment in cases of Poisoning, &c. For the use of Amateurs. By HUGH DALZIEL. Second Edition. *In paper, price* 1s.; *in cloth gilt,* 2s.

DUCKS AND GEESE: Their Characteristics, Points, and Management. Splendidly Illustrated. *In paper, price* 1s. 6d.

EXHIBITION ACCOUNT BOOKS. For use at all Dog, Poultry, Rabbit, and Cage Bird Shows. In Four Books, comprising: I. Minute Book; II. Cash Book; III. Entries Book; IV. Ledger. With Full Directions, and Illustrative Examples for Working them. N.B.—The Set of Four Books is kept in Three Series: No. 1, for Show of 500 Entries, 5s. the Set; No. 2, for 1000 Entries, 7s. 6d. the Set; and No. 3, for 1500 Entries, 12s. 6d. the Set. Larger sizes in proportion. The books can be had separate. MINUTE BOOK—No. 1, 1s.; No. 2, 1s. 3d.; No. 3, 2s. CASH BOOK—No. 1, 2s.; No. 2, 2s. 6d.; No. 3, 4s. ENTRIES BOOK—No. 1, 2s.; No. 2, 2s. 6d.; No. 3, 4s. Ledger—No. 1, 2s.; No. 2, 2s. 6d.; No. 3, 4s.

FANCY WORK SERIES, ARTISTIC. A Series of Illustrated Manuals on Artistic and Popular Fancy Work of various kinds. Each number is complete in itself, and issued at the uniform *price* of 6d. Now ready—(1) MACRAMÉ LACE (Second Edition); (2) PATCHWORK; (3) TATTING; (4) CREWEL WORK; (5) APPLIQUÉ; (6) FANCY NETTING.

FERNS, CHOICE BRITISH. Descriptive of the most beautiful Variations from the common forms, and their Culture. By C. T. DRUERY, F.L.S. Very accurate PLATES, and other Illustrations. *In cloth gilt, price* 2s. 6d.

FERRETS AND FERRETING. Containing Instructions for the Breeding, Management, and Working of Ferrets. Second Edition, Re-written and greatly Enlarged. Illustrated. *In paper, price* 6d.

FERTILITY OF EGGS CERTIFICATE. These are Forms of Guarantee given by the Sellers to the Buyers of Eggs for Hatching, undertaking to refund value of any unfertile eggs, or to replace them with good ones. Very valuable to sellers of eggs, as they induce purchases. *In books, with counterfoils, price* 6d.

FIREWORK-MAKING FOR AMATEURS. A most complete, accurate, and easily understood work on Making both Simple and High-class Fireworks. By Dr. W. H. BROWNE, M.A. *Price* 2s. 6d.

FOREIGN BIRDS, AMATEUR'S AVIARY OF; or, How to Keep and Breed Foreign Birds with Pleasure and Profit in England. Illustrated. By W. T. GREENE, M.D., M.A., F.Z.S., F.S.S., &c., Author of "Parrots in Captivity," &c. *In cloth gilt, price* 3s. 6d.

FOX TERRIER, THE. Its History, Points, Breeding, Rearing, Preparing for Exhibition, and Coursing. By HUGH DALZIEL. Illustrated. *Price* 1s.

☞ **All Books Post Free.**

GAME AND GAME SHOOTING, NOTES ON. Miscellaneous Observations on Birds and Animals, and on the Sport they afford for the Gun in Great Britain, including Grouse, Partridges, Pheasants, Hares, Rabbits, Quails, Woodcocks, Snipe, and Rooks. By J. J. MANLEY, M.A. Illustrated. *In cloth gilt*, 400*pp., price* 7*s.* 6*d.*

GAME PRESERVING, PRACTICAL. Containing the fullest Directions for Rearing and Preserving both Winged and Ground Game, and Destroying Vermin; with other Information of Value to the Game Preserver. Illustrated. By WILLIAM CARNEGIE. *In cloth gilt, demy* 8*vo, price* 21*s.*

GARDENING, DICTIONARY OF. A Practical Encyclopædia of Horticulture, for Amateurs and Professionals. Illustrated with upwards of 2240 Engravings. Edited by G. NICHOLSON, Curator of the Royal Botanic Gardens, Kew; assisted by Prof. Trail, M.D., Rev. P. W. Myles, B.A., F.L.S., W. Watson, J. Garrett, and other Specialists. *In* 4 *vols., large post* 4*to.* Vol. I., A to E, 552pp., 743 Illustrations; Vol. II., F to O, 544pp., 811 Illustrations; Vol. III., P to S, 537pp., 564 Illustrations; Vol. IV., T to Z, and Supplement of Pronouncing Dictionary, Indices to Plants for Special Purposes, Recent Introductions, &c. 322 Illustrations. *Price* 15*s. each.*

GARDEN PESTS AND THEIR ERADICATION. Containing Practical Instructions for the Amateur to overcome the Enemies of the Garden. With numerous Illustrations. *In paper, price* 1*s.*

GOAT, BOOK OF THE. Containing Full Particulars of the various Breeds of Goats, and their Profitable Management. With many Plates. By H. STEPHEN HOLMES PEGLER. Third Edition, with Engravings and Coloured Frontispiece. *In cloth gilt, price* 4*s.* 6*d.*

GOAT-KEEPING FOR AMATEURS: Being the Practical Management of Goats for Milking Purposes. Abridged from "The Book of the Goat," by H. S. HOLMES PEGLER. Illustrated. *In paper, price* 1*s.*

GREENHOUSE MANAGEMENT FOR AMATEURS. Descriptions of the best Greenhouses and Frames, with Instructions for Building them, particulars of the various methods of Heating, Illustrated Descriptions of the most suitable Plants, with general and special Cultural Directions, and all necessary information for the Guidance of the Amateur. Second Edition, Revised and Enlarged. Magnificently Illustrated. By W. J. MAY. *In cloth gilt, price* 5*s.*

GREYHOUND, THE: Its History, Points, Breeding, Rearing, Training, and Running. By HUGH DALZIEL. With Coloured Frontispiece. *In cloth gilt, demy* 8*vo, price* 2*s.* 6*d.*

GUINEA PIG, THE, for Food, Fur, and Fancy. Illustrated with Coloured Frontispiece and Engravings. An exhaustive book on the Varieties of the Guinea Pig, and its Management. By C. CUMBERLAND, F.Z.S. *In cloth gilt, price* 2*s.* 6*d.*

☙ **All Books Post Free.**

HANDWRITING, CHARACTER INDICATED BY. With Illustrations in Support of the Theories advanced taken from Autograph Letters of Statesmen, Lawyers, Soldiers, Ecclesiastics, Authors, Poets, Musicians, Actors, and other persons. Second Edition. By R. BAUGHAN. *In cloth gilt, price* 2s. 6d.

HARDY PERENNIALS and Old-fashioned Garden Flowers. Descriptions, alphabetically arranged, of the most desirable Plants for Borders, Rockeries, and Shrubberies, including Foliage as well as Flowering Plants. Profusely Illustrated. By J. WOOD. *In cloth, price* 5s.

HORSE-KEEPING FOR AMATEURS. A Practical Manual on the Management of Horses, for the guidance of those who keep them for their personal use. By FOX RUSSELL. *Price* 1s.

HORSES, DISEASES OF: Their Causes, Symptoms, and Treatment. For the use of Amateurs. By HUGH DALZIEL. *In paper, price* 1s.

JOURNALISM, PRACTICAL: How to Enter Thereon and Succeed. A Manual for Beginners and Amateurs. A book for all who think of "writing for the Press." By JOHN DAWSON. *In cloth gilt, price* 2s. 6d.

LEGAL PROFESSION, A GUIDE TO THE. A Practical Treatise on the various Methods of Entering either Branch of the Legal Profession ; also a Course of Study for each of the Examinations, and selected Papers of Questions ; forming a Complete Guide to every Department of Legal Preparation. By J. H. SLATER, Barrister-at-Law, of the Middle Temple. *Price* 7s. 6d.

LIBRARY MANUAL, THE. A Guide to the Formation of a Library and the Valuation of Rare and Standard Books. By J. H. SLATER, Barrister-at-Law. Second Edition. *In cloth, price* 2s. 6d.

LILY OF THE VALLEY: All About It, and How to Grow It ; Forced Indoors and Out of Doors, in Various Ways. By WILLIAM ROBERTS. *In paper covers, price* 6d.

MEDITERRANEAN WINTER RESORTS. A Practical Handbook to the Principal Health and Pleasure Resorts on the Shores of the Mediterranean. By E. A. R. BALL. With a Map and 27 Illustrations. *Fcap. 8vo, price* 3s. 6d.

MICE, FANCY: Their Varieties, Management, and Breeding. Re-issue, with Criticisms and Notes by DR. CARTER BLAKE. Illustrated. *In paper, price* 6d.

MODEL YACHTS AND BOATS: Their Designing, Making, and Sailing. Illustrated with 118 Designs and Working Diagrams. A splendid book for boys and others interested in making and rigging toy boats for sailing. It is the best book on the subject now published. By J. DU V. GROSVENOR. *In leatherette, price* 5s.

All Books Post Free.

MONKEYS, NOTES ON PET, and How to Manage Them. Profusely Illustrated. By ARTHUR PATTERSON. *Cloth gilt, price* 2s. 6d.

MUSHROOM CULTURE FOR AMATEURS. With Full Directions for Successful Growth in Houses, Sheds, Cellars, and Pots, on Shelves, and Out of Doors. Illustrated. By W. J. MAY. *In paper, price* 1s.

NATURAL HISTORY SKETCHES among the Carnivora — Wild and Domesticated; with Observations on their Habits and Mental Faculties. By ARTHUR NICOLS, F.G.S., F.R.G.S. Illustrated. *In cloth gilt, price* 5s.

NEEDLEWORK, DICTIONARY OF. An Encyclopædia of Artistic, Plain, and Fancy Needlework; Plain, practical, complete, and magnificently Illustrated. By S. F. A. CAULFEILD and B. C. SAWARD. Accepted by H.M. the Queen, H.R.H. the Princess of Wales, H.R.H. the Duchess of Edinburgh, H.R.H. the Duchess of Connaught, and H.R.H. the Duchess of Albany. Dedicated by special permission to H.R.H. Princess Louise, Marchioness of Lorne. *In demy 4to, 528pp., 829 Illustrations, extra cloth gilt, plain edges, cushioned bevelled boards, price* 21s.; *with COLOURED PLATES, elegant satin brocade cloth binding, and coloured edges,* 31s. 6d.

ORCHIDS FOR AMATEURS. Containing Descriptions of Orchids suited to the requirements of the Amateur, with full Instructions for their successful Cultivation. A New and Enlarged Edition, edited by W. WATSON, Assistant Curator, Royal Botanic Gardens, Kew, *in demy 8vo, with COLOURED PLATES*, in the Press.

PAINTING, DECORATIVE. A Practical Handbook on Painting and Etching upon Textiles, Pottery, Porcelain, Paper, Vellum, Leather, Glass, Wood, Stone, Metals, and Plaster, for the Decoration of our Homes. By B. C. SAWARD. *Cheap Edition, price* 5s.

PARROTS, THE SPEAKING. The Art of Keeping and Breeding the principal Talking Parrots in Confinement. By Dr. KARL RUSS. Illustrated with COLOURED PLATES and Engravings. *In cloth gilt, price* 5s.

PATIENCE, GAMES OF, for one or more Players. A very clearly-written and well-illustrated Book of Instructions on How to Play no less than FORTY different Games of Patience. By Miss WHITMORE JONES. Illustrated. Second Edition. *Price* 1s.

PERSPECTIVE, THE ESSENTIALS OF. With numerous Illustrations drawn by the Author. By L. W. MILLER, Principal of the School of Industrial Art of the Pennsylvania Museum, Philadelphia. This book is such a manual as has long been desired for the guidance of art students and for self-instruction. The instructions are clearly set forth, and the principles are vividly enforced by a large number of attractive drawings. *Price* 6s. 6d.

∴ **All Books Post Free.**

PHEASANT-KEEPING FOR AMATEURS. A Practical Handbook on the Breeding, Rearing, and General Management of Fancy Pheasants in Confinement. By GEO. HORNE. Illustrated with Diagrams of the necessary Pens, Aviaries, &c., and a COLOURED FRONTISPIECE and many full-page Engravings of the chief Varieties of Pheasants, drawn from life by A. F. LYDON. *In cloth gilt, price 3s. 6d.*

PIANOFORTES, TUNING AND REPAIRING. The Amateur's Guide to the Practical Management of a Piano without the intervention of a Professional. By CHARLES BABBINGTON. *In paper, price 6d.*

PICTURE FRAME MAKING FOR AMATEURS. Being Practical Instructions in the Making of various kinds of Frames for Paintings, Drawings, Photographs, and Engravings. Illustrated. By the Author of "Carpentry and Joinery," &c. Cheap Edition, *in paper, price 1s.*

PIG, BOOK OF THE. Containing the Selection, Breeding, Feeding, and Management of the Pig; the Treatment of its Diseases; the Curing and Preserving of Hams, Bacon, and other Pork Foods; and other information appertaining to Pork Farming. By Professor JAMES LONG. Fully Illustrated with Portraits of Prize Pigs, by HARRISON WEIR and other Artists, Plans of Model Piggeries, &c. *In cloth gilt, price 10s. 6d.*

PIGEONS, FANCY. Containing Full Directions for the Breeding and Management of Fancy Pigeons, and Descriptions of every known Variety, together with all other information of interest or use to Pigeon Fanciers. Third Edition, bringing the subject down to the present time. 18 COLOURED PLATES, and 22 other full-page Illustrations. By J. C. LYELL. *In cloth gilt, price 10s. 6d.*

POKER BOOK, THE. A Practical Book on Playing the Fascinating Game of Draw Poker with Success. *Price 1s.*

POULTRY FOR PRIZES AND PROFIT. Contains: Breeding Poultry for Prizes, Exhibition Poultry, and Management of the Poultry Yard. Handsomely Illustrated. New Edition, Revised and Enlarged. By Professor JAMES LONG. *In cloth gilt, price 3s. 6d.*

RABBIT, BOOK OF THE. A Complete Work on Breeding and Rearing all Varieties of Fancy Rabbits, giving their History, Variations, Uses, Points, Selection, Mating, Management, &c., &c. NEW EDITION, Revised and Enlarged. Edited by KEMPSTER W. KNIGHT. With an additional chapter on "Hutch Rabbit Farming in the Open," by MAJOR MORANT. Illustrated with Coloured and other Plates. *One handsome vol., price 15s.*

RABBITS FOR PRIZES AND PROFIT. Containing Full Directions for the Proper Management of Fancy Rabbits in Health and Disease, for Pets or the Market, and Descriptions of every known Variety, with Instructions for Breeding good specimens. Illustrated. By CHARLES RAYSON. *In cloth gilt, price 2s. 6d.* Also as follows :—

❦ All Books Post Free.

Rabbits, General Management of. Including Hutches, Breeding, Feeding, Diseases and their Treatment, Rabbit Coverts, &c. Fully Illustrated. *In paper, price 1s.*

Rabbits, Exhibition. Being descriptions of all Varieties of Fancy Rabbits, their Points of Excellence, and how to obtain them. Illustrated. *In paper, price 1s.*

REPOUSSÉ WORK FOR AMATEURS: Being the Art of Ornamenting Thin Metal with Raised Figures. By L. L. HASLOPE. Illustrated. *In cloth gilt, price 2s. 6d.*

ROSES FOR AMATEURS. A Practical Guide to the Selection and Cultivation of the best Roses, both for Exhibition or mere Pleasure, by that large section of the Gardening World, the Amateur Lover of Roses. Illustrated. By the REV. J. HONYWOOD D'OMBRAIN, Hon. Sec. of the National Rose Society. *Price 1s.*

ST. BERNARD, THE. Its History, Points, Breeding, and Rearing. By HUGH DALZIEL. Illustrated. *Demy 8vo, cloth, price 2s. 6d.*

SEA-FISHING FOR AMATEURS. Practical Instructions to Visitors at Seaside Places for Catching Sea-Fish from Pier-heads, Shore, or Boats, principally by means of Hand Lines, with a very useful List of Fishing Stations, the Fish to be caught there, and the Best Seasons. By FRANK HUDSON. Illustrated. *Crown 8vo, price 1s.*

SEASIDE WATERING PLACES. A Description of nearly 200 Holiday Resorts on the Coasts of England and Wales, the Channel Islands, and the Isle of Man, including the gayest and most quiet places, giving full particulars of them and their attractions, and all other information likely to assist persons in selecting places in which to spend their Holidays according to their individual tastes; with BUSINESS DIRECTORY of Tradesmen, arranged in order of the Towns. Sixth Edition. Illustrated. *In cloth, price 2s. 6d.*

SHEET METAL, WORKING IN: Being Practical Instructions for Making and Mending Small Articles in Tin, Copper, Iron, Zinc, and Brass. Illustrated. Third Edition. By the Rev J. LUKIN, B.A. *In paper, price 6d.*

SHORTHAND, ON GURNEY'S SYSTEM (IMPROVED), LESSONS IN: Being Instruction in the Art of Shorthand Writing as used in the Service of the two Houses of Parliament. By R. E. MILLER. *In paper, price 1s.*

SHORTHAND SYSTEMS; WHICH IS THE BEST? Being a Discussion, by various Experts, on the Merits and Demerits of all the principal Systems, with Illustrative Examples. Edited by THOMAS ANDERSON. *In paper, price 1s.*

SICK NURSING AT HOME: Being Plain Directions and Hints for the Proper Nursing of Sick Persons, and the Home Treatment of Diseases and Accidents in case of Sudden Emergencies. By S. F. A. CAULFEILD. *In paper, price 1s.; bound in cloth, price 1s. 6d.*

※ **All Books Post Free.**

SKATING CARDS: An Easy Method of Learning Figure Skating, as the Cards *can be used on the Ice. In cloth case*, 2s. 6d., or *in strong leather pocket book, price* 3s. 6d.; *or in extra calf, satin lined, price* 5s. 6d.

SLEIGHT OF HAND. A Practical Manual of Legerdemain for Amateurs and Others. New Edition, Revised and Enlarged. Profusely Illustrated. By E. SACHS. *Cloth gilt*, 6s. 6d.

SNAKES, MARSUPIALS, AND BIRDS: A Book of Anecdotes, Adventures, and Zoological Notes. A capital Book for Boys. By ARTHUR NICOLS, F.G.S., F.R.G.S., &c. Illustrated. *Price* 5s.

TAXIDERMY, PRACTICAL. A Manual of Instruction to the Amateur in Collecting, Preserving, and Setting-up Natural History Specimens of all kinds. Fully Illustrated with Examples and Working Diagrams. By MONTAGU BROWNE, F.Z.S., Curator of Leicester Museum. Second Edition. *In cloth gilt, price* 7s. 6d.

THEATRICALS AND TABLEAUX VIVANTS FOR AMATEURS. Giving Full Directions as to Stage Arrangements, " Making-up," Costumes, and Acting. With Numerous Illustrations. By CHAS. HARRISON. *In cloth gilt, price* 2s. 6d.

TOURIST'S ROUTE MAP of England and Wales, The. Third Edition, thoroughly Revised. Shows clearly all the Main, and most of the Cross, Roads, and the Distances between the Chief Towns, as well as the Mileage from London. In addition to this, Routes of *Thirty of the most Interesting Tours* are printed in red. The Map is mounted on linen, and is the fullest, handiest, and best tourist's map in the market. *In cloth, price* 1s..

TOYMAKING FOR AMATEURS. Containing Instructions for the Home Construction of Simple Wooden Toys, and of others that are Moved or Driven by Weights, Clockwork, Steam, Electricity, &c. Illustrated. By JAMES LUKIN, B.A. *In cloth gilt, price* 4s.

TRAPPING, PRACTICAL: Being some Papers on Traps and Trapping for Vermin, with a Chapter on General Bird Trapping and Snaring. By W. CARNEGIE. *In paper, price* 1s.

TURNING FOR AMATEURS: Being Descriptions of the Lathe and its Attachments and Tools, with Minute Instructions for their Effective Use on Wood, Metal, Ivory, and other Materials. New Edition, Revised and Enlarged. By JAMES LUKIN, B.A. Illustrated with 144 Engravings. *In cloth gilt, price* 2s. 6d.

VINE CULTURE FOR AMATEURS: Being Plain Directions for the Successful Growing of Grapes with the Means and Appliances usually at the command of Amateurs. Illustrated. Grapes are so generally grown in villa greenhouses that this book cannot fail to be of great service to many persons. By W. J. MAY.

VIOLIN SCHOOL, PRACTICAL, for Home Students. A Practical Book of Instructions and Exercises in Violin Playing, for the use of Amateurs, Self-learners, Teachers, and others With a Supplement on " Easy Legato Studies for the Violin." By J. M. FLEMING. 1 *handsome vol., demy* 4to, *half-Persian, price* 9s. 6d.

☜ **All Books Post Free.**

12 *Published by* L. UPCOTT GILL, 170, *Strand, London, W.C.*

WATERING PLACES OF FRANCE, NORTHERN.
A Guide for English People to the Holiday Resorts on the Coasts of the French Netherlands, Picardy, Normandy, and Brittany. By ROSA BAUGHAN. *In paper, price* 2s.

WOOD CARVING FOR AMATEURS. Containing Descriptions of all the requisite Tools, and Full Instructions for their Use in producing different varieties of Carvings. Illustrated. A book of very complete instructions for the amateur wood carver. *In paper, price* 1s.

London : L. UPCOTT GILL, 170, Strand, W.C.

Crown 8vo, cloth, with Illustrations, Price 5s.
WORKSHOP RECEIPTS,
FOR THE USE OF MANUFACTURERS, MECHANICS, AND SCIENTIFIC AMATEURS.
By ERNEST SPON.

Crown 8vo, cloth, 5s.
WORKSHOP RECEIPTS
(SECOND SERIES).
By ROBERT HALDANE.
Devoted mainly to subjects connected with Chemical Manufactures. An entirely New Volume. Uniform in Size, Style, and Type with the Original "Workshop Receipts."

Crown 8vo, cloth, 5s.
WORKSHOP RECEIPTS
(THIRD SERIES).
By C. G. WARNFORD LOCK, F.L.S.
Devoted mainly to Electrical and Metallurgical Subjects.

Crown 8vo, cloth, 5s.
WORKSHOP RECEIPTS
(FOURTH SERIES).
By C. G. WARNFORD LOCK, F.L.S.
Devoted mainly to Handicrafts and Mechanical Subjects.
250 *Illustrations, with Complete Index, and a General Index to the Four Series.*

Demy 8vo, cloth, 6s.
SPONS' MECHANIC'S OWN BOOK:
A Manual for Handicraftsmen and Amateurs, complete in one large vol., containing 700pp. and 1420 Illustrations. Second Edition.
CONTENTS:
Mechanical Drawing; Casting and Founding in Iron, Brass, Bronze, and other Alloys; Forging and Finishing Iron; Sheet-metal Working; Soldering, Brazing, and Burning; Carpentry and Joinery, embracing descriptions of some 400 Woods, over 200 Illustrations of Tools and their Uses, Explanations (with Diagrams) of 116 Joints and Hinges, and Details of Construction of Workshop Appliances, Rough Furniture. Garden and Yard Erections, and House-Building; Cabinet-Making and Veneering; Carving and Fretcutting; Upholstery; Painting, Graining, and Marbling; Staining Furniture, Woods, Floors, and Fittings; Gilding, Dead and Bright, on various grounds; Polishing Marble, Metals, and Wood; Varnishing; Mechanical Movements, illustrating contrivances for transmitting Motion; Turning in Wood and Metals; Masonry, embracing Stonework, Brickwork, Terra-cotta, and Concrete; Roofing with Thatch, Tiles, Slates, Felt, Zinc, etc.; Glazing with and without Putty, and Lead Glazing; Plastering and Whitewashing; Paperhanging; Gas-fitting; Bell-hanging, ordinary and electric systems; Lighting; Warming; Ventilating; Roads, Pavements, and Bridges; Hedges, Ditches, and Drains; Water Supply and Sanitation; Hints on House Construction suited to New Countries.

London: E. & F. N. SPON, 125, Strand.

BOOKS PUBLISHED BY HORACE COX,

AT THE "FIELD" OFFICE, 346, STRAND, LONDON, W.C.

FOURTH EDITION. *In post 8vo, limp cloth, gilt, price 2s. 6d., by post 2s. 8d.*

THE ART OF SKATING; With Illustrations, Diagrams, and Plain Directions for the Acquirement of the Most Difficult and Graceful Movements. By GEORGE ANDERSON ("Cyclos"), Vice-President of the Crystal Palace Skating Club, and for many years President of the Glasgow Skating Club.

THIRD EDITION. *Price 7s. 6d., by post 7s. 10d.*

FIGURE SKATING; Being the Theory and Practice of the Art as Developed in England, with a Glance at its Origin and History. By H. C. VANDERVELL and T. MAXWELL WITHAM (Members of the London Skating Club). There are thousands of skaters who attain a small amount of skill in Figure Skating, and there stop, because they neither know what to do, or how to do it. A reference to this, the acknowledged Text Book of Figure Skating, will solve any difficulty that may have stopped progress for years. It now includes all the new Figures, with the new nomenclature which has been authorised by the Skating Club.

Price 8d., by post 9d.

THE "FIELD" LAWN TENNIS UMPIRES' SCORE-SHEET BOOK (Sixty Sets), with Instructions for the Use of Umpires. Adapted for the Use of Umpires, as used at the Championship Meetings.

FOURTH EDITION. *In demy 4to, on toned paper, and in fancy cover, price 2s., by post 2s. 2d.*

THE BOOK OF DINNER SERVIETTES contains a New Introduction on the Decoration of Dinner Tables, and General Directions for Folding the Serviettes. There are Twenty-one different kinds given, with Ninety-two Woodcuts illustrative of the various Folds required and the Serviettes complete.

Demy 8vo, price 5s. 6d., by post 5s. 10d.

THE ROTHAMSTED EXPERIMENTS ON THE GROWTH OF WHEAT BARLEY, AND THE MIXED HERBAGE OF GRASS LAND. By WILLIAM FREAM, B.Sc. Lond., F.L.S., F.G.S., F.S.S.

In demy 8vo, price 3s. 6d., by post 3s. 9d.

HINTS ON THE MANAGEMENT OF HAWKS. By J. E. HARTING, Author of "A Handbook of British Birds," "Essays on Sport and Natural History."

Price 1s., by post 1s. 2d. With Full-Page Coloured Illustration and Woodcuts.

PALLAS'S SAND GROUSE: Its Natural History, and a Plea for its Preservation. By W. B. TEGETMEIER.

THE RULES OF PIGEON SHOOTING. Published by Special Permission; the Hurlingham Club and the Gun Club Rules of Pigeon Shooting. SECOND EDITION. Bound together in cloth, gilt edges, price 6d., by post 7d.

THE LAWS OF LAWN TENNIS, as adopted by the Marylebone Cricket Club and the All England Croquet and Lawn Tennis Club. Entered at Stationers' Hall. Price 6d., by post 6½d.

"FIELD" OFFICE,
346, STRAND, LONDON, W.C.

SOME BOOKS FOR ANGLERS

PUBLISHED BY

SAMPSON LOW, MARSTON AND CO.

WALTON AND COTTON'S COMPLEAT ANGLER.

The Lea and Dove Illustrated Edition. Being the One Hundredth Edition of Walton and Cotton's ever-popular work, "The Compleat Angler." Edited, with Lives of Walton and Cotton, by R. B. MARSTON, Editor of the *Fishing Gazette*, Hon. Treasurer of the Fly Fishers' Club, &c., and containing a Reprint (by permission) of "The Chronicle of the Compleat Angler," being a Bibliographical Record of its various Editions and Imitations. By THOMAS WESTWOOD and THOMAS SATCHELL. The principal feature of this Edition will be a set of fifty-four Full-page Photogravures, printed from Copper Plates, on fine plate paper, of Views on the Lea, Dove, &c.

EDITION DE LUXE, in 2 vols., royal 4to, each copy numbered and signed, to Subscribers £10 10s. nett.

The DEMY QUARTO EDITION, bound in half morocco, gilt top, £5 5s. nett.

"The noblest gift-book that has been issued for many years."—*St. James' Gazette.*
"Never has Walton been more honoured. . . . Among collectors, therefore, there is no question but that the book will be attractive. It will be one of the forms in which the work of Walton will be most coveted."—*Standard.*
"These sumptuous volumes."—*Spectator.* "A truly magnificent edition."—*Field.* "This noble edition."—*Daily News.*

READY IN THE SPRING.

DRY FLY FISHING IN THEORY AND PRACTICE.

By FREDERIC M. HALFORD, F.L.S., Author of "Floating Flies and How to Dress Them," "Detached Badger" of the *Field*, Member of the "Houghton Club," "Fly Fishers' Club," &c. An *Edition de Luxe*, limited to 100 copies, and the First Edition of 500 copies, are in preparation, and will be published this season. Illustrated with Plates showing the Position of the Rod and Line in making various Casts used in Dry Fly Fishing; also Coloured and other Plates, giving the Life History of the Mayfly; a Coloured Plan showing how the Weeds in a River should be Cut, &c., &c.

CONDITIONS OF PUBLICATION.

Edition de Luxe, imperial octavo, printed on the best English hand made paper, bound in full morocco, with gilt top, with the plates on mounts. Limited strictly to 100 copies. *Each copy will be numbered and signed.* Price per copy. Subscribers, £2 2s.

First Edition, royal octavo, printed on the finest printing paper, cloth extra, 500 copies. Price per copy, Subscribers, £1 5s.

N.B.—All Coloured Illustrations are hand-coloured in both Editions, except the plans illustrating Chapters IV. and XIII.

FLOATING FLIES AND HOW TO DRESS THEM. A

Treatise on the most Modern Methods of Dressing Artificial Flies for Trout and Grayling. With full Illustrated Directions, and containing ninety Hand-coloured Engravings of the most Killing Patterns, together with a few Hints to Dry-fly Fishermen. By FREDERIC M. HALFORD, "Detached Badger" of *The Field*, Member of the Houghton Club, Fly-fishers' Club, &c. Second edition, demy 8vo, cloth, 15s., post free.

        "Of Blue Duns and Bumbles, of hooks and their eyes,
        Of Red Tags and Coachmen, and all sorts of flies:
        Of Wickhams, Red Spinners, and others, ne'er failing
        To lure out of water the trout and the grayling—
        Here Halford discourses, and shows a collection
        Of ninety fly-portraits, all limned to perfection:
        A capital volume, and no one will doubt it,
        No fisherman now should be ever without it!"—*Punch.*

NEAR AND FAR: an Angler's Sketches of Home Sport and

COLONIAL LIFE. By WM. SENIOR ("Red Spinner"), Angling Editor of *The Field*, Author of "Waterside Sketches," &c. Crown 8vo, cloth, 6s.

"The author is not merely an expert all round angler, but is an all-round lover of nature; and he hast he vouch happy faculty of knowing how to describe what he sees and what he has done. He has fished, and shot, and hunted, and communed with nature the world over; and he describes his adventures with a lightness and brightness of touch which to anyone who has in him the least love of nature cannot but be irresistibly charming."—*Fishing Gazette.*

TO ANGLERS.—If you do not know the paper, send a post-card to the Manager of THE FISHING GAZETTE, St. Dunstan's House, Fetter Lane, London.

TO ANGLERS.—"The Fishing Gazette"

is Devoted entirely to Angling, and gives, every Saturday, Original Articles, Reports from Rivers, Clubs, Correspondence; and has a Splendid Show of Advertisements from leading Fishing Tackle Makers, Fishing Hotels, &c.

TO ANGLERS.—Send for a LIST OF BOOKS ON ALL KINDS OF ANGLING to Manager of THE FISHING GAZETTE, St. Dunstan's House, Fetter Lane, London.

ROWLANDS' TOILET ARTICLES

Have been known for nearly 100 years to be the best which can be obtained; the best articles are, in the long run, always the cheapest.

ROWLANDS' MACASSAR OIL

Is the best and safest preserver and beautifier of the hair, and has a most delicate and fragrant bouquet. It contains no lead or mineral ingredients, and can also be had in

A GOLDEN COLOUR

for fair and golden-haired children, and people whose hair has become grey. Sizes: 3/6, 7/-; 10/6, equal to four small.

ROWLANDS' KALYDOR

Is a most soothing emollient and refreshing preparation for the face, hands, and arms. It removes all freckles, tan, sunburn, sting of insects, prickly heat, chaps, redness, irritation and roughness of the skin, &c., produces a beautiful and delicate complexion, and renders the

SKIN SOFT, FAIR,

and delicate; it is warranted free from any greasy or metallic ingredients. Sizes: 4/6 and 8/6. *Half-sized bottles at 2/3.*

ROWLANDS' ODONTO

Is the best, purest, and most fragrant Tooth Powder; it prevents and arrests decay, strengthens the gums, gives a pleasing fragrance to the breath, and renders the

TEETH WHITE AND SOUND.

ROWLANDS' EUKONIA

Is a pure and delicate toilet powder, free from any bismuth or metallic ingredients. Sold in three tints, white, rose, and cream, 2/6 per box. Ask for

ROWLANDS' ARTICLES,

of 20, HATTON GARDEN, LONDON, and avoid cheap, spurious imitations, under the same or similar names.

BY SPECIAL APPOINTMENT.

Purveyors by Special Warrants to
H.M. THE QUEEN
and
H.R.H. THE PRINCE OF WALES.

BY SPECIAL APPOINTMENT.

SPRATTS PATENT
Meat "Fibrine" Vegetable
DOG CAKES
(WITH BEETROOT).

BEWARE OF WORTHLESS IMITATIONS!
SEE EACH CAKE IS STAMPED
SPRATTS PATENT and a "X."

COD LIVER OIL
DOG CAKES.
For Puppies after Distemper, and for Dainty Feeders and Sick or Pet Dogs.

DISTEMPER POWDERS, WORM POWDERS, MANGE, ECZEMA, and EAR CANKER LOTIONS, TONIC CONDITION PILLS, &c.

PAMPHLET ON CANINE DISEASES,
And full List of Medicines, Post Free.

Dog, Poultry, & Game Houses & Appliances.

TO POULTRY REARERS.

SPRATTS PATENT
POULTRY MEAL.
The Most Nutritious and Digestible Food for Chicks and Laying Hens (being thoroughly cooked). Samples Post Free.

New Edition of "**THE COMMON SENSE of POULTRY KEEPING**," 3d., Post Free.

GRANULATED PRAIRIE MEAT, "CRISSEL."
Price 25s. per cwt. Takes the Place of Insect Life.

"CARDIAC;" A TONIC FOR POULTRY.
Price 1s. per Packet, or 3s. per 7lb. Bag.

GAME MEAL.
SAMPLE AND FULL PARTICULARS POST FREE.

Extract from "THE FIELD":—"Thanks to Spratts Pheasant Meal and Crissel, I have reduced the cost a great deal, and reared a considerably greater average. With Spratts Food they require no custards, ants' eggs, or, in fact, anything from hatching till they are turned in coverts and eat corn."—CAREFUL SPORTSMAN.

"**The Common Sense of Pheasant Rearing**," 3d., Post Free.

Spratts Patent, Limited, London, S.E.

www.ingramcontent.com/pod-product-compliance
Lightning Source LLC
Chambersburg PA
CBHW031411160426
43196CB00007B/977